COMMUNICATE FOR SUCCESS

COMMUNICATE FOR SUCCESS

How to Manage, Motivate, and Lead Your People

ERIC SKOPEC

▲▼▼ **Addison-Wesley Publishing Company, Inc.**

Reading, Massachusetts   Menlo Park, California   New York
Don Mills, Ontario   Wokingham, England   Amsterdam
Bonn   Sydney   Singapore   Tokyo   Madrid   San Juan

Library of Congress Cataloging-in-Publication Data

Skopec, Eric W., 1946–
    Communicate for success : how to manage, motivate, and lead your
    people / Eric Skopec.
        p.   cm.
    Includes bibliographical references.
    ISBN 0-201-10528-4
    1. Communication in management. 2. Employee motivation.
3. Industrial management.   I. Title.
HD30.3.S56   1990   90-32052
658.4'5 – dc20   CIP

Text design by Cameron Olson
Typeset in 11 pt. Helvetica
Typeset by Neil W. Kelley

ISBN 0-201-10528-4

ABCDEFGHIJ–MA–9543210
First printing, March 1990

Contents

Preface   ix

Introduction   1

Rewards for Success   2

Challenges   2

Where We Stand   4

Becoming a Manager   5

The Traditional Approach   7

Leading: Managing Through Communication   9

Building Relationships   9

Essential Skills   10

Communication Styles as Habits   11

Scoring the Communication Style Inventory   11

Four Primary Communication Styles   13

Strengths and Weaknesses of the Communication Styles   15

Choosing Communication Styles   17

Plan of This Book   18

Suggested Readings   19

Case Studies   20

Chapter 1: Selecting Subordinates   27
Mark's Problem   28
A Common Problem   29
What You Need to Know   32
Preparing an Interview Guide   35
Analyzing Applicants' Credentials   40
Conducting Thoughtful Interviews   45
Making the Selection   50
Conclusion   53
Suggested Readings   54
Case Study   55

Chapter 2: Coaching and Delegation   61
Learning to Delegate   63
The Manager's Role   66
You Can't Get There from Here   68
Delegation and Coaching Defined   69
Job Expectancy Scale   71
Delegation and Coaching with the Job
    Expectancy Scale   74
Working with Teams   76
Conclusion   82
Suggested Readings   83
Case Studies   84

Chapter 3: Overcoming Performance
Problems   91
The Anatomy of Performance Problems   93
A General Theory of Motivation   94
Employees' Motives   95
Organizational Mission   96
Opportunities to Achieve   98
Performance Problem One: The Lazy Subordinate   100
Performance Problem Two: The Hostile Subordinate   101
Performance Problem Three: Ineffective Teams   102
Personal Development Conferences   103

Team Building: Leading a Work Group   107
Conclusion   110
Suggested Readings   112
Case Study   113

Chapter 4: Appraising Subordinate Performance   117

Common Problems   119
Avoiding the Problems   121
Audiences for Performance Appraisal   122
Appraisal Strategies   124
Providing Feedback   128
Coping with Criticism   131
Responding to Difficult Behaviors   132
Conducting the Interview   133
Conclusion   135
Suggested Readings   136
Case Study   137

Chapter 5: Interpersonal Negotiation and Influence   141

Opportunities to Negotiate   142
New Opportunities for Negotiation   142
Approaches to Conflict   147
Values and Limitations   148
An Approach to Negotiation   151
Before the Negotiation Session   151
Conduct During the Negotiation Session   154
Concluding the Negotiation Session   157
Tools of the Trade: Some Negotiation Tactics   159
A Closing Note: Power and Politics in Organizations   161
Conclusion   162
Suggested Readings   164
Case Studies   165

**Chapter 6:   The End of the Road:
                Managing Terminations   173**
Termination Interviews   176
Exit Interviews   182
Conclusion   186
Suggested Readings   188
Case Study   189

Index   193

Preface

I've really enjoyed my career in management. In fact, I can't think of anything I would rather have done with my life. However, there is one thing I would change. If I had the chance to do it all again, I wouldn't waste so much time learning about things. Instead, I'd get right down to business and start fresh learning how to work with people. The ability to work with people is what really counts.

This manager's sentiments reflect the feelings of many experienced executives looking back on their careers. Statistics, finance, marketing research, accounting, and strategic planning all have their places. But we know today that they contribute little to a person's ability to work with others in constructive and creative ways.

The ability to manage, motivate, and lead is far more important than any of the technical skills. Being a manager means working with people, and working with people requires refined communication skills.

Readers of this book will identify their own communication styles, and they will learn to recognize strengths and weaknesses in their own communication and in the communication of others. They will then learn specific communication skills needed to hire skilled and dedicated people, delegate work and coach subordinates, manage performance problems, conduct effective performance appraisals, negotiate with employees and others, and conduct exit and termination interviews.

These activities are the heart and soul of management. The lessons of experience and common sense point to the same conclusion: If you expect to be a successful manager, you need to be an effective communicator.

As you read this book, you will share some of my experiences and you will share in the experiences of countless other managers with whom I have worked. They come from many fields—engineering, accounting, hotel and restaurant management, communications, medical management, transportation, public utilities, and financial services management, to name just a few. Many have been remarkably successful, and all have been anxious to share their solutions to everyday problems. You will meet many of these managers in the following pages, and you may benefit from their experiences.

An Instructor's Guide is available from:

Editorial Department
Corporate and Professional Group
Addison-Wesley Publishing Company
Reading, MA 01867

Introduction

This is an exciting time for anyone pursuing a career in management. Rewards, in the form of compensation, visibility, and opportunity, have never been greater. At the same time, barriers to success have never been higher. Competitive business environments, changing employee expectations, and new ways of organizing businesses place new emphasis on communication. While few managers have developed the needed skills—witness the breakdowns compromising many firms—self-directed learning techniques introduced in this book make it relatively easy to master sophisticated approaches.

This chapter introduces an expanded view of communication and gives readers an opportunity to identify their personal communication styles. Traditional writing and formal speaking skills are still important, but meeting today's challenges demands skill in developing and maintaining relationships. Relationships, in turn, depend on open communication established by soliciting information from others, presenting one's own views without creating unnecessary hard feelings, and discussing behaviors. These skills are the foundation of the specific managerial tasks described in the rest of the book.

This is an exciting time for anyone interested in management. Rewards for success have never been greater.

Rewards for Success

Compensation packages have reached levels that were unheard of just a few years ago. A recent survey showed the average salary for managers in large corporations is over $70,000. Six-figure salaries are common and annual compensation figures in the millions are reported regularly.

Public visibility is another reward for success. Senior managers regularly appear in the media. Polls show that some are better known than many candidates for political office—even better known than some presidential candidates.

A third reward for success in management is the ability to get things done. Today's managers control resources that didn't exist just a decade ago. And they have used these resources to accomplish things of which few people even dream. They have put men on the moon, rebuilt major corporations, and turned computers into practical home appliances. Tomorrow promises to be just as exciting.

Challenges

While the rewards have never been greater, becoming a successful manager has gotten harder. In fact, it is probably harder today than at any time in the past. Let's look at some of the things that make it tough.

More and more companies work in highly competitive environments. Foreign competition especially has forced everyone to be "sharper." As a result, the demands for performance have never been greater. A few organizations still reward seniority, but most look for concrete evidence of accomplishment. Whereas yesterday's manager could expect to be promoted just for putting in time, few companies now can afford to keep managers who don't produce. Management by objectives, periodic reviews, and pay for performance are a few of the devices developed to reinforce the link between performance and reward.

As if increased demands for performance weren't enough to make managers lose sleep, there have been dramatic changes in the kinds of work they do. Managers work through other people to get things done, but the expectations of those people—the employees—are very different from those of yesterday. Many employees used to be satisfied with clearly defined work rules. They expected managers to tell them what to do and often appreciated the assurance of knowing someone else was responsible for the job.

Of course there were always a few workers who were not satisfied with limiting conditions. They were a minority, and even dissatisfied workers lacked the vocabulary to ask for more options. Their demands were limited to higher salaries and more fringe benefits.

Today's employees expect to have far more active roles. They expect to participate in decisions affecting production, and they no longer respond to orders as earlier generations did. The majority expect their supervisors to explain tasks and responsibilities. They expect their managers to reason with them when disagreements arise. And they expect to grow as a result of their assignments.

While employees' expectations have been changing, so has the kind of work they do. Just a generation ago, many employees were confined to production lines. Little initiative was required. Managers' jobs often consisted of seeing that employees were at the right place at the right time. "Motivation" meant little more than reducing absenteeism. Managers at all levels could rely on authority to "keep the line running."

The use of teams is the single most important development in American management over the last few decades. Company after company is adopting team structures and it is important to note that they aren't doing it because the Japanese or anyone else is doing it. Teams are becoming popular because they provide enormous competitive advantages for the firms that use them.

It doesn't make sense to ask whether or not the team concept will work. The evidence that it does is overwhelming. The only interesting question is whether or not companies that don't use teams will survive.
—A management consultant

Today, assembly lines are reminders of a bygone era. Where they are still used, employees are often organized in production teams with broad responsibility for maintaining the line, scheduling production, and monitoring their own performance. Even "paper pushing" tasks have been relegated to computers, and employees at every level are expected to display initiative.

Yesterday's suggestion boxes have been replaced by quality circles, and employees may be asked to help solve even major corporate problems. People power is part of the slogan at many corporations, and news stories frequently tell of employees' contributions to successful organizations.

Where We Stand

These changes—today's highly competitive environment, new employee expectations, and altered working conditions—have affected managers at every level. From first-line supervisors to corporate officers, the nature of managerial work has changed dramatically. And with this change, the skills required for success have changed. While yesterday's managers could rely on technical knowledge and authority to get things done, today's managers need to rely on interpersonal skills. Even "tough bosses" need people committed to high performance.

Expanded technical knowledge can be gained through work assignments and discussions in team meetings, where members can learn from each other—particularly when everybody feels free to share the problems and issues of subareas. But the managerial and interpersonal skills pose the greatest obstacle in this system. Lack of technical knowledge is seldom the reason that a person above the rank of supervisor fails to perform. Performance difficulties usually arise from the "softer" and more touchy issues of how to motivate others, handle conflict and disagreements, make and meet commitments, conduct meetings, and use influence. The most frequently mentioned reason (except for economic staff reduction) in numerous surveys conducted by recruiting firms for why managerial-rank personnel lose their jobs is that the person in some way "didn't get along well."
—David L. Bradford and Allan R. Cohen, *Managing for Excellence* (New York: John Wiley & Sons, 1984), p. 76.

While changes in the nature of managerial work have highlighted the role of communication, there is alarming evidence that many managers are not skilled in this area. The studies summarized below show what can go wrong.

In one company, 91 percent of top officers knew that profits were declining. They didn't do a very good job of telling others; only 48 percent of upper-middle managers, 21 percent of managers at the next level, and 5 percent of first-line supervisors knew about the problem.

In another study, participants had difficulty communicating even basic information about their jobs. Six months after explaining ways to reduce the problem, the researcher returned to find that managers and subordinates in nine pairs said they had not discussed the problem. Both members of six pairs agreed that they had discussed the problem. Members of seven pairs could not agree on whether or not they had discussed the problem.

Supervisors and their subordinates in another company used diaries to keep track of their on-the-job communication. At the end of the study, supervisors reported giving an average of 165 clear directions to each subordinate while the subordinates reported receiving an average of only 84. In other words, almost half of the instructions "got lost" or misinterpreted.

Seventy-five percent of foremen in another study said they "always" or "almost always" got ideas from subordinates before trying to solve work-related problems. Only 16 percent of the workers agreed.

Forty percent of the workforce in the United States doubts the truth of what management tells them.

We could point to many more studies that show the same thing. Many managers are not effective communicators. "But," you might ask, "how did they get to be managers if they cannot communicate effectively?" To answer that question, let's take a brief look at how someone gets to be a manager.

Becoming a Manager

Very few people are hired as managers. Most begin as technicians—people working with things. They are hired as technicians because they are good at doing something. Usually, that something doesn't require effective communication. John Smith is as good an example as any.

At 52, John is a senior manager in the microelectronics research division of a major corporation. He is responsible for seven major projects with a combined annual budget of over 35 million dollars. More than 100 employees work in his group with seven project managers and five staff directors reporting directly to him. As you can imagine, John spends a lot of time managing people. The box on this page shows John's typical work day.

A DAY IN THE LIFE OF JOHN SMITH

8:00   Meet with Administrative Assistant to review day's schedule; dictate offer letters to two candidates for jobs

8:20   Weekly status meeting with seven Project Managers

9:45   Meeting continues in private with two Project Managers and Director of Computing Services

11:00 Brief meeting with Human Resources Manager to review current searches and examine two applicants' credentials

11:20 Read project and budget status reports

12:00 Lunch with applicant for Project Manager position

1:25   Telephone calls to colleagues who are familiar with applicant's work history

1:45   Review notes for presentation to new employees

2:30   Attend orientation meeting for new employees

3:45   Return telephone calls

4:30   Conduct six-month performance review of Budget Manager

5:25   Phone conference with Human Resources Manager and two Staff Managers who interviewed applicant for Project Manager position

5:45   Read draft of annual report to corporate headquarters; note to Administrative Assistant to arrange meetings with Project and Staff managers who are over budget

6:30   Leave for home

Looking at his responsibilities, you may be surprised to learn that John has never taken a management course. He has no formal training in working with people. John is an electrical engineer and often wishes that people were as dependable as the things he studied in college.

After graduating from college, John worked as a junior engineer, designing control systems for an automobile manufacturer. The work was boring and repetitive; John mastered it quickly. When three new engineers were hired the following year, John was asked to "keep an eye on them." Capitalizing on this managerial experience, he jumped to another company where he became a "lead" engineer. His boss retired a couple of years later and John was "bumped up" to become a junior project manager. That may not sound like much of a title, but it was all John needed. He has been a manager ever since.

As a manager, John has experienced a few setbacks. Fortunately, he has never had a major disaster. Most of his projects have been successful—he often worked long hours when he couldn't count on others to get things done. His salary and responsibilities grew every year for quite a while. He had a pretty good start, but things have gotten tougher the last few years.

John has recently begun to feel like he is "losing it." The "it" is his ability to manage his division—and he may be right. The union has singled out his division for several job actions. Worse yet, he has had trouble keeping good technicians and subordinate managers. Promising employees stay just long enough to get some experience and then transfer to other divisions. Sometimes, he says, it seems like the offices have revolving doors. To top things off, John is overdue for promotion. The problems have damaged his record and it looks like he is stuck—managing seven major projects and over 100 people with no place to go. And the job is getting harder every day because, he says, he "just doesn't understand what these people want." "These people" are his subordinates—the people who work for him and now seem to spend most of their time making his life difficult.

The Traditional Approach

John's story has a lot in common with many others. In fact, almost all managers begin as John did. They start out as promising technicians and then get moved into management when they develop a reputation for getting things done. Unfortunately, many people never notice how they get things done. Too often they got things done by pushing their subordinates to the limit—and beyond! And when the subordinates couldn't keep up, they did the job themselves.

Many of today's managers got a lot done this way. No one can really blame them for using this approach. Their bosses used it, and it was often the only approach they were allowed to use. And even more important, it worked. In fact, it worked pretty well—at least until recently.

As the amount of competition grew, the nature of the work changed, and the expectations of the employees evolved, the traditional approach no longer worked quite so well. These changes caught many managers off guard. All of a sudden, the approaches that used to work very well simply stopped working. Describing traditional managers' problems is a good starting point for understanding newer approaches to management.

Management used to be pretty easy. You made the right moves and you knew what the payoffs would be. Today, it's like a game without any rules. Sometimes you win, sometimes you lose—but you never know why.
—Quotation from a frustrated manager

Not having enough time or energy to get everything done is the number one complaint of traditional managers. Even working long hours—50, 60, or even 70 hours a week—traditional managers never seem to get everything done.

The time problem is often compounded by their number two problem: There is nobody they can count on. Traditional managers often find themselves alone when there are tough problems to solve. Their subordinates never seem to have the intelligence, initiative, or common sense to solve problems on their own.

Finally, traditional managers often find that they are indispensable. That may not sound like a problem, but it is when you look down the road. These managers are so important that the system simply stops working whenever they are out of the office. As a result, they seldom have time for themselves or their families—they are always on call psychologically, even when they don't wear a beeper. Vacations are nearly impossible and, worse yet, promotions are out of the question because there is no one else who can do the job.

Although working managers often see the three problems as separate concerns, consultants and scholars recognize them as symptoms of a more fundamental problem; traditional managers never make full use of the human resources available to them. Because they try to do everything themselves, they virtually never have enough time or energy to get everything done. Even when they delegate work to their subordinates, they are likely to delegate specific tasks without explaining how these tasks contribute to the overall effort.

It doesn't take long for most subordinates to read the handwriting on the wall: Traditional managers control everything and no one else is given an opportunity to grow or develop. Ambitious employees learn what they can and move on as quickly as possible. Remaining employees respond just the way you might expect. They display little initiative and rely on the manager for everything. Is it any wonder that traditional managers are always on call and usually so vital that they cannot be promoted?

Leading: Managing Through Communication

Fortunately, there is another approach to management. Managers can be leaders, developing, nurturing, and using the human talent around them. This approach has been described in several influential books. *The One Minute Manager, Reinventing the Corporation, In Search of Excellence, Peak Performers, Thriving on Chaos,* and *The Art of Being a Boss* all describe managers who are at peace with themselves and with those around them. These are managers who have the ability to get the best from the people with whom they work. In a word, these are managers who can *communicate.* By reading this book, you have taken an important step toward joining their ranks.

As we have learned more about successful managers, we have learned more about the kinds of communication that are needed. Making presentations, writing reports, composing memos, and crafting tactful letters are all important. No one can afford to overlook these activities for long. But we now know that some other kinds of communication are even more important. Outstandingly successful managers are very good at establishing mutually satisfying relationships.

Building Relationships

The emphasis on establishing and maintaining relationships is probably the single most important finding of recent research on management. We used to think that the most important part of being a manager involved technical activities. We used words like "analyzing," "planning," "controlling," and "directing" to describe what managers do. Now we realize that managers usually don't have enough power or authority to do any of these things without first establishing good relationships with the people who work for and around them.

Over the years, I've seen lots of bright young men and women move into management. That step always demands growth and it is never an easy one. I don't know what the academic research says but I know from experience that some make it and some don't. The one thing that seems to make a difference is how well a new manager gets along with his or her people. If the relationship is good, they can learn whatever they have to. If the relationship is bad, no amount of technical skill can make up the difference.
—An experienced manager

John Kotter, a Harvard professor, found that successful general managers have hundreds, or even thousands, of personal relationships. They have personal relationships with the people who work for them, with the people they work for, with other people in similar jobs, with customers and suppliers, and with other people in their industry. These relationships make it possible for managers to get things done; the communication skills they use to establish and maintain these relationships are essential qualifications for success.

Essential Skills

Successful managers are successful, at least in part, because they are skilled communicators. They are skilled at getting information from others; they are able to express their own views without creating hard feelings, even on controversial subjects; and, they are skilled at discussing behavior. The essential skills are relatively easy to develop and you will see them modeled throughout this book. But just having these skills isn't enough. The hard part is knowing when and how to use them.

In the last few years, researchers have begun to focus on when and how managers use essential communication skills. We now know that everyone has a characteristic communication style. This style is a basic or fundamental approach to communicating that shows up in just about everything a person says or does. Before reading about common communication styles, you may want to complete the test on the next page. After filling out this communication style inventory, continue reading to see how to interpret your results.

Communication Styles as Habits

Communication styles are like many other behaviors. As we mature, we learn first to communicate with the people closest to us. These are often members of our families. With age we come into contact with many other people; friends, playmates, teachers. Each person we meet can teach us something new about ourselves and our approach to communication. Eventually, the rate at which we learn new things begins to slow and we get set in our habits.

As long as our surroundings remain the same, our habits are likely to serve us as well as they did when we first learned them. But as our surroundings change, the habits may not work as well as they once did. This doesn't mean that the habits are wrong; in fact it doesn't make much sense to talk about right or wrong. However, it does mean that we need to develop new habits to cope with new surroundings.

The transition to management is one of the most significant changes most of us will ever make. Those who were lucky enough to grow up in a setting that encouraged appropriate habits are likely to seem blessed. Others who grew up in less favorable circumstances are likely to find the transition more difficult. Developing an appropriate communication style may be the single most critical step in becoming an effective manager.

Scoring the Communication Style Inventory

The first step in scoring the communication style inventory is checking your work. In each row, make sure that you have scored 8 for the response most like you, 4 for the second response, 2 for the third, and 1 for the response least like you.

After you have checked your work, add up the numbers in each column. Your total for each column is your score for a particular communication style. To identify your characteristic communication style, compare your scores to the averages displayed in Figure I.1.

Communication Style Inventory

Alan J. Rowe, Tom J. Housel, Eric Skopec © 2/22/88, Rev. 10/20/88

Instructions

Place an 8, 4, 2, or 1 after each response to the 20 questions. The number *cannot* be repeated. 8 is used for the response that is most like you. 4 is one that is somewhat less. 2 is for the response that is a little like you and 1 is for the response that is least like you. There is no time limit, so please respond carefully.

1. I prefer to communicate:	by phone		in writing		to a group		one-on-one
2. In social gatherings, I:	talk to others		listen to what is said		discuss many things		enjoy the conversation
3. I explain things:	very quickly		based on factual data		based on my knowledge		based on my feelings
4. I express my ideas best:	orally		on paper		telling stories		talking about my experiences
5. To convince others I'm right, I:	speak forcefully		use logical arguments		explain my reasoning		speak gently
6. When confronted by others, I:	become defensive		answer them back		try to smooth things out		avoid arguing
7. I describe others:	objectively		factually		using generalities		favorably
8. People say I speak:	assertively		carefully		thoughtfully		in a patient manner
9. When making a suggestion, I:	tell others what I think		am very specific		point out consequences		try to be helpful
10. When I'm not sure what to say, I:	rely on my experience		search for information		consider what's best		ask for advice
11. When I reject a request, I:	am firm		rely on policies		show concern		try to be pleasant
12. I always try to:	get results		solve problems		explore new ideas		talk with others
13. When under stress, I:	talk rapidly		become cautious		speak anxiously		ask for help
14. If I am late, I:	say what comes to mind		look for an excuse		apologize		avoid the subject
15. When talking to others, I:	speak first		cover many details		discuss ideas		make them feel good
16. When I write, I:	am brief		am factual		am descriptive		mention people
17. I enjoy reading:	adventure stories		technical books		historic novels		about people
18. In business meetings, I:	speak my mind		observe what's happening		think about what is said		listen to others
19. I learn best when given:	basic facts		supporting theory		explanations		examples of what to do
20. When questioning others, I:	come directly to the point		ask them for backup data		want complete answers		consider their feelings

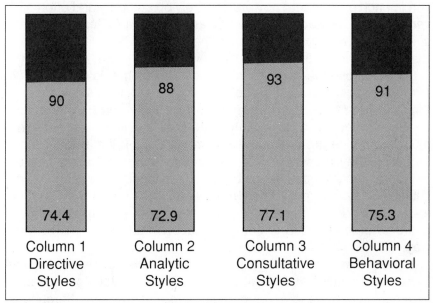

Figure I.1   Average communication style scores

Your characteristic communication style is represented by the column or columns where your score is above the average. Scores well above the averages (in the black zones on each bar) represent dominant communication styles. Most people have one dominant style that represents their most common approach to communication. In addition, most people have one and occasionally two backup communication styles. Backup styles are represented by scores slightly above the average (in the grey zones on each bar). Backup styles are approaches to communication that are used when a person chooses not to use their dominant style.

Now let's look at the communication styles and see when each is most appropriate.

Four Primary Communication Styles

Scores above the average in the first column represent a *directive* communication style. People who score high in this column usually approach communication as a one-way activity. They seldom ask questions and almost never pause for other people to "get a word in." People with a directive style also provide relatively little information in each exchange. They prefer to rely on authority and often give very specific directions to subordinates. They also tend to expect subordinates to follow directions to the letter and have little tolerance for people who do things their own way.

Scores above the average in the second column point to an *analytic* communication style. People who score high in this column also approach communication as a one-way activity and frequently expect subordinates to do exactly what they are told. Analytic communicators differ from directive communicators in the amount of information they present. Whereas directive communicators rely on authority, analytic communicators rely on superior knowledge of the subject. They frequently know more about the subject than anyone else—or at least they think they do—and use overwhelming amounts of information to convince subordinates to do things their way.

Scores above the average in the third column identify a *consultative* communication style. Like analytic communicators, consultative communicators use large amounts of information. The difference is that people with consultative styles think of communication as a two-way activity. Whereas analytic communicators appear to give

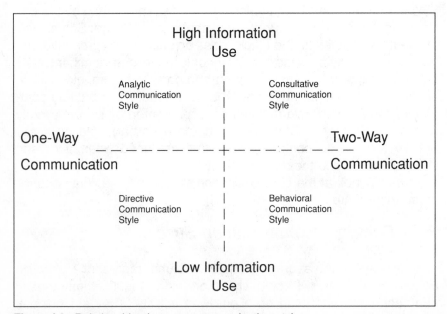

Figure I.2. Relationships between communication styles

speeches, consultative communicators participate in extended conversations. They often display considerable skill as participants in group discussions. They use information to help members of the group find mutually acceptable solutions, not to dominate other members of a group. When giving directions to subordinates, they are usually content to explain the purpose or direction of activity and let subordinates figure out the best way to get things done.

Scores in the fourth column indicate a *behavioral* communication style. Like consultative communicators, behaviorals approach communication as a two-way activity and are usually skilled at involving others. They differ from consultative communicators in contributing relatively little information to the conversation. They focus on the behavior of the participants and are usually more concerned with developing relationships than with accomplishing any task.

Relationships between these four communication styles are shown in Figure I.2.

Strengths and Weaknesses of the Communication Styles

Each of the four communication styles has particular strengths and weaknesses. There is no simple right or wrong, but each style works well in some situations and not so well in others.

The directive style is characteristic of traditional managers, and you can probably guess what its weaknesses are. Because subordinates are given specific directions with few opportunities to do things their own way, they have little reason to develop initiative or responsibility. Directive managers hold the reins, and subordinates are never given a chance to grow or develop their own skills.

Although a directive style has many weaknesses, there are some cases when it can be used effectively. Directive styles are best when time is so limited or risks so great that unquestioning obedience is required. Directive styles may also be appropriate when dealing with unskilled employees in situations where initiative is neither expected nor desired. Finally, directive styles may also be used when the manager has such complete power over employees that there is no reason to experiment with other approaches.

Analytic styles have many of the weaknesses of directive styles. Because communication is primarily one-way and because the manager expects the subordinate to follow instructions to the letter, subordinates don't have an opportunity to develop their own approaches. The fact that analytic communicators use large quantities of information adds another variable. Because presenting information takes time, analytic communicators lose the advantage of speed. However, there are cases in which an analytic style is most appropriate. It is an ideal approach to educating new workers who benefit from the information presented. The analytic style is also a useful way of persuading or influencing others when a manager does not have sufficient power or authority simply to give orders.

Consultative and behavioral styles are preferred by nontraditional managers because they allow subordinates to develop and test their own approaches. This contributes to subordinates' feelings of ownership and encourages them to exercise higher levels of initiative. These are desirable qualities, and there are few cases in which managers should choose not to develop them.

Although both consultative and behavioral styles encourage subordinate growth, there are some differences between them. Because consultative communicators present large quantities of information, they are particularly helpful when subordinates encounter task-related problems. However, when subordinates encounter problems focusing on relationships, behaviorals are less likely to cause defensive reactions.

The difference between task-related problems and problems involving relationships is an important concept. To make sure you're comfortable with the difference, take a minute to look at some of the problems Karen, an administrative assistant, faces in a typical day.

Karen is responsible for scheduling frequent meetings between her boss, Marilyn Jones, and several other executives. The task consumes a great deal of time, and Karen generally likes to get it out of the way early in the day. Most of the executives she contacts are cooperative but four cause particular problems: Fred Smith is getting ready for a lengthy trip and would like to postpone the meeting with Marilyn until he returns. Paula Ortiz is attending an out-of-town convention and won't return for ten days. Mark Johnson has been away from his desk and hasn't returned Karen's calls even though she has left several messages. Finally, Karen has avoided calling Sharon Lewis because things got a little heated the last time they talked. Karen had been trying to set up a meeting but Sharon responded as if she thought Karen were giving her orders. "I don't work for you, young lady, and I will schedule my own meetings if you don't mind!" was her angry response.

Even with this brief description, it is easy to see that these executives represent different kinds of problems. Their schedules make it hard for Karen to arrange meetings with Fred Smith and Paula Ortiz. These are clearly task-related problems.

Sharon Lewis presents a problem of a different sort. Her attitude seems inappropriate but she may have been responding to something Karen said or to other pressures. In any case, Karen's reluctance to call points to a relationship problem.

Finally, we don't have enough information to know whether Mark Johnson presents a task or relationship problem. He may not have gotten his messages—a task problem—or he may have decided not to return Karen's calls—a relationship problem.

If Marilyn is on her toes, she will deal with these problems in different ways. She will use a consultative style to tell Karen how to schedule appointments with Fred and Paula. Marilyn may even fall back on a directive style if she is pressed for time and not worried about her relationship with Karen. If Karen is in control emotionally, Marilyn should also use a consultative style to tell Karen how to deal with Mark Johnson. However, if Karen is becoming angry or frustrated, Marilyn should choose a behavioral style just as she will to help Karen deal with her feelings toward Sharon Lewis.

Here is the easiest way to keep the difference in mind. If a subordinate doesn't know what to do, a task-related problem exists, and the manager should use a consultative style to teach. On the other hand, if the subordinate knows what to do but is avoiding it, most likely there is a relationship problem, and the manager should use a behavioral style to help the subordinate cope with his or her feelings.

Choosing Communication Styles

Communication styles are like many other behaviors—each works well in some situations. An analytic style, for example, may work well when a professor talks to a student. However, using an analytic style may not work nearly as well when planning an outing with a friend. The same is true of all styles. What works in one situation may have disastrous consequences in another.

From a managerial point of view, the important thing is recognizing when your normal style is likely to cause problems and shifting to

another style. Fortunately, communication styles are like all behaviors—we learned to use a particular communication style and we
can learn to use others when it is important to us.

Many of the cases in this book call attention to communication
styles and suggest alternate styles that may be more appropriate.
As you work through each case, ask yourself what style the participants seem to be using. Try to anticipate the consequences of using
that style. And ask yourself what you would try instead. When time
permits, put yourself in the role of the participants and practice using
each of the styles. You will probably find that some styles seem
more natural than others. That is a normal reaction. The styles with
which you are least comfortable are probably the ones you use least
often. Learning to use those styles can be a big step in your personal
and professional development.

Plan of This Book

In the chapters that follow, we will show you how to use communication skills to do many of the things a manager needs to do every
day. Chapter One will show you what skills to use in hiring new
employees, and Chapter Two will show how to use related skills in
delegating tasks and responsibilities. Chapter Three will show how
to deal with performance problems, and Chapter Four shows how
performance appraisals can be made positive, rewarding experiences. Chapter Five introduces negotiation techniques, and Chapter
Six shows how to use termination and exit interviews to end an
employment relationship.

Case studies and related materials—presented at the end of each
chapter—play a special role in this text. Each has been chosen or
developed to highlight particular themes from the chapter and to
give you an opportunity to test your problem-solving skills. For example, the case studies at the end of this chapter describe four typical
managers as seen by the people who know them well. As you review
these case studies, you will see how important communication styles
can be, and the kinds of problems that may arise when a manager
uses an inappropriate style.

Suggested Readings

Badway, M. K. "Why Managers Fail." *Research Management* 26 (May–June 1983): 26–31.

Bradford, David L., and Allan R. Cohen. *Managing for Excellence.* New York: John Wiley & Sons, 1984.

Drucker, Peter. *Management.* New York: Harper and Row, 1974.

Eisenbeis, H. Richard. "The Role of Technical Professionals in Management." *Industrial Management* 29 (March–April 1987): 13–17.

Gabarro, John J. "When a New Manager Takes Charge." *Harvard Business Review* (May–June 1985): 110–123.

Kotter, John P. *The General Managers.* New York: The Free Press, 1982.

Mintzberg, Henry. *The Nature of Managerial Work.* New York: Harper and Row, 1973.

Odiorne, George S. *How Managers Make Things Happen.* 2d ed. Englewood Cliffs, New Jersey: Prentice-Hall, 1982.

Case Studies

The following case studies describe four typical managers. The descriptions are composites of the managers as seen by the people who know them best—their friends and coworkers.

As you read each description, try to identify the manager's communication style. You may also be able to figure out what the managers do well and what kinds of situations may cause them problems. The analytical guide following the case studies will help you evaluate your analyses.

Marsha Jones

"I worked for Marsha for nine years. I guess I got to know her just like she was a member of my family. In fact, I have never worked for a warmer or more caring person. She always seemed to have time to listen to other people's problems, even when they had nothing to do with work. One incident really stands out in my mind.

"We had been working on a major project for about six months and had fallen a month behind schedule. Everyone was working long hours trying to catch up. Marsha was working fourteen-hour days, including Saturdays and Sundays. Even with that pressure, there was no doubt that she was ready to help with our personal problems. Maybe that's why everyone was willing to work so hard.

"I'm still not sure what went wrong. Even though we were working long hours, we weren't able to get the project back on track. Marsha was always there with us but things never got any better. Other groups got extra help when they fell behind schedule, but we never did. Marsha explained that we were short-handed, but the company never paid much attention to her.

"Eventually, she was replaced by a new guy who got everything he wanted. The project got finished in record time, and it was kind of exciting to watch everything fall into place. But, I still miss talking to Marsha."

Mark Howard

Mark is the rising star in his company. He has an undergraduate degree in physics from a state university and an M.B.A. from a leading business school. He is careful and precise, and he doesn't make decisions without thinking about all of the implications. People in the company say he has never made a mistake, and his project summaries show that he is doing an outstanding job.

In meetings, Mark avoids speaking until he is sure of himself. He may listen to everyone else first, but everybody knows that it is time for a speech when he gets started. He never seems to forget anything and he can remember even small details of projects he worked on five or six years ago. Few people disagree with him anymore because everyone knows that he can win almost any argument—he simply overwhelms everyone else with details.

Mark doesn't seem to have any flaws, but some people call him a cold fish. A secretary who worked for him last year says that she left because "he never really cared about me—or about anyone else as far as I can tell." Mark's boss says that "he is one of the most promising people in the division. I just wish he would learn to give simple yes and no answers when someone asks a question."

Karen Smith

Karen is an experienced hotel manager with a reputation for getting things done. She moves around quite a bit because her employer often gives her clean-up assignments. That means that she doesn't have a permanent home, and she has arranged her personal life so she can move whenever the company calls on her.

She has few close friends, she says, "because few people move as fast as I do—I just can't stand to sit around waiting for someone else to make a decision."

Karen has a great professional track record and she has helped her company bail out five hotels in the last six years. That is an impressive record by any standard, but Karen is modest about her achievement. "I don't really know why people make such a big deal about my record," she says. "Everything is so simple when you know what to look for. I just pick out the weak links and lean on them until they shape up or move on."

Karen's boss describes her as "a real dynamo. I have never known anyone else who could get so much done so fast," he says. Then he adds, "Of course she had some problems when she first started working for us. Really our fault, I think. We made the mistake of leaving her at one place too long, and several key people there left the company because of her. But, as I say, that was really our fault— we just had to figure out the best way to use her."

Richard Martin

Ask his employees and they will all say pretty much the same thing: "Dick is one of the best people I've ever worked for. He knows more about this business than anyone else I've ever seen. But he never puts other people down—even when they have it coming. He is a good listener and always seems to have time for other people."

That is a very positive description, and you would have to work hard to get his coworkers to say anything negative about Dick. Even his boss shares the positive feelings, but he recognizes one weakness. "I'm worried about the future," he says, "because Dick hasn't learned how to make a decent presentation. No matter what the subject or who he is talking to, Dick always begins by asking questions. Don't get me wrong—I know there are times when you need to get your audience involved and I know that asking questions is one way to bring them into the presentation. It's just that you can't always take the time. We had a real problem last year when Dick was supposed to present a proposal to our Board of Directors. We had worked for four and a half months, and Dick knew the material inside and out. The Board had set aside forty minutes for the presentation but had gotten off schedule and cut our time to ten minutes. I told Dick that the Board was sure to accept the proposal—all he needed to do was hit the high points. He said he understood and I still don't know why he didn't follow through. When it came time for him to speak, he started by asking each Board member what he or she thought of the proposal. I cut him off after the fifth question and asked him to summarize the main points. He said OK but then got sidetracked discussing the history of the proposal. The Chairman stopped him after twenty-five minutes of ancient history, and it took us six months to get another chance to make our pitch. We eventually got the Board's approval but we lost a lot of time, and I'm afraid Dick's career got set back quite a bit."

Analytical Guide

Marsha Jones: behavioral style; popular with employees but appears unable to influence company officials

Mark Howard: analytical style; cold and distant in dealing with employees; expect motivation and retention problems unless he "warms up"

Karen Smith: directive style; good at getting things done but not at building relationships or developing people

Richard Martin: consultative style; skilled at developing relationships and involving audiences but may be inflexible and unable to adapt to unexpected situations

1

Selecting Subordinates

Recruiting and developing dedicated, skilled, and creative employees should be a major part of every manager's job. Although most large firms use Personnel or Human Resources departments—alone or in conjunction with outside employment agencies—managers should never delegate final responsibility for selecting employees. In fact, since the next decade will be marked by shortages of skilled employees, managers will need to be more active than ever before in selecting and recruiting new employees.

Faced with some potential employees, managers need to find out who has the required technical skills, who will perform well in the working environment, and what will be necessary to hire each candidate. Placement interviews are commonly used to make these decisions but research indicates that untrained managers make serious errors. Untrained managers talk too much, rely on first impressions, fail to follow up on inconsistent answers, and get unreliable information. The resulting errors cost corporations millions of dollars every year. The human costs—anger, frustration, and poor performance— are even greater.

This chapter shows how to structure selection interviews to avoid common errors. You will learn to analyze resumés and credentials, set a climate encouraging honesty and openness, ask appropriate legal questions, actively listen to answers, follow up (probe) incomplete answers, and make reasoned decisions with the information gathered.

Mark's Problem

Arriving at work on Wednesday morning, Mark found an "URGENT" message from his boss, Joan. She planned to be in her office all morning, the note said, and wanted to see him immediately.

The tone of Joan's message was unusually cold. Mark had a good idea why she was anxious to see him. He was responsible for the software development segment of a project, and his group hadn't been able to keep up. As a result, the whole project was five months behind schedule and there was growing pressure to get back on track.

When his group had started falling behind, Mark had discussed the problem with Joan, and she had authorized him to hire three new programmers. That, Mark told himself, was when things really began to go downhill.

Mark had called Personnel and asked them to line up interviews with five or six programmers. He planned to choose the best and call in others if he didn't like what he saw.

Unfortunately, there were only four applications on file, and the chief recruiter thought it would take at least two months to locate and screen additional candidates. The news got worse; of the four applicants, one had already taken a job elsewhere and another had decided to go back to school.

Personnel arranged interviews for Mark with the two remaining applicants. John, the first interviewee, really seemed to know his stuff and Mark was very comfortable with him. The second interviewee, Louise, was rather shy and reserved. Mark didn't like her, but he was in a hurry and decided to offer jobs to both John and Louise.

Secretly, Mark was pleased when only John accepted the job offer. Although Mark was still short-handed, he was confident that John could pick up some of the load and help him keep things together while Personnel located more applicants.

Now, two months later, Personnel still hadn't identified any candidates with the necessary skills, and John had become a major disappointment. In fact, he had only added to the problems. During his first week on the job, he had alienated just about everyone he was supposed to work with. Two of the senior programmers on the project had told Mark that they would quit rather than work with John. Worse yet, John's work was so sloppy that Mark found himself spending more time checking it for errors than in doing his own work.

Things had reached the breaking point yesterday, and Mark had called John into his office for a heart-to-heart conversation. They hadn't even gotten into the tough issues, in Mark's mind, when John announced that he didn't have to take this stuff and stormed out of the office. Minutes later, Personnel called to tell Mark that John had submitted his resignation and was threatening legal action.

Now Mark was really stuck. He still didn't have the programmers he needed, his group was falling further and further behind, two of the senior programmers were questioning his ability, and Joan seemed to be losing patience with him.

A Common Problem

Mark's problem was more extreme than most, but many managers face similar dangers. Statistics show that there aren't enough skilled workers to go around, and the situation is likely to get worse in the next few years. The problems will be greatest in high-tech industries, and firms in the rapidly growing service sector will also experience difficulties.

As the baby boom ages, and the baby bust enters the workforce, the average age of the workforce will climb from 36 today to 39 by the year 2000. The number of young workers age 16–24 will drop by almost 2 million, or 8 percent. This decline in young people in the labor force will have both positive and negative impacts. On the one hand, the older workforce will be more experienced, stable, and reliable. The reverse side of this stability will be a lower level of adaptability. Older workers, for example, are less likely to move, to change occupations, or to undertake retraining than younger ones. Companies that have grown by adding large numbers of flexible, lower-paid young workers will find such workers in short supply in the 1990s.
—William B. Johnston and Arnold H. Packer, *Workforce 2000* (Indianapolis, Indiana: Hudson Institute, 1987), pp. xix–xx.

As a result, managers at all levels and in all parts of the economy will find themselves on the front lines—screening and recruiting new employees.

Personnel and/or Human Resources departments will face a big part of the task. They will be responsible for finding and screening applicants. Many departments will rely on outside agencies. Head-hunters will become even more popular. But even the best of the agencies will be hard-pressed to find enough qualified applicants to meet the demands.

As these problems emerge, managers will find they have to become ever more involved in recruiting and selecting employees. Even with the help of Personnel and Human Resources departments, and with the guidance of outside agencies, managers will decide who gets hired. And, the ability to find and hire the right people will become a key factor affecting managers' careers.

Most managers will rely on interviews to make hiring decisions. Unfortunately, interviews are imprecise tools and many managers lack skills needed to conduct effective interviews. Even the best intentioned managers may slant their questions and distort the interviewing process. A candidate who makes a good first impression is often treated very differently from one who doesn't. For example, applicants for a clerical position might be asked a series of questions about their knowledge of computers. Those making a good first impression might be engaged in the following conversation:

INTERVIEWER: What word processing programs do you use?

INTERVIEWEE: At school we learned Wordperfect.

INTERVIEWER: I see. Have you ever used Wordstar?

INTERVIEWEE: A little—but not very much.

INTERVIEWER: That's OK. I'm sure you can learn quickly, can't you?

Other applicants, those who did not make good first impressions, might be treated very differently.

INTERVIEWER: What word processing programs do you use?

INTERVIEWEE: At school we learned Wordperfect.

INTERVIEWER: I see. You know that we only use Wordstar in this office.

INTERVIEWEE: Well, uh . . . I suppose I could learn.

INTERVIEWER: I'm sorry, we just don't have time to train someone.

It's easy to see what a great impact first impressions can have.

The sad thing is that unskilled interviewers make the same mistakes again and again. They talk too much, rely on first impressions, ask loaded questions, overlook evidence of problems, and get unreliable information. All too often, the wrong people get hired and both companies and their employees suffer.

During the 1970s, the cost of replacing dissatisfied employees who left in their first few months on the job was estimated at more than eleven billion dollars per year in this country. Just counting the effects of inflation, the costs are probably much higher today.

Nobody wins if you don't take interviews seriously. Managers can get stuck with careless, unskilled, uncaring employees interested only in their paychecks. Employees run the risk of being pushed into jobs that don't match their skills or interests, and seeing their careers permanently damaged. The way I see it, interviews are hard work, but cutting corners hurts everyone.
—An experienced manager

Researchers have identified the kinds of errors unskilled interviewers are most likely to make. The good news is that researchers have also devised ways to avoid these errors. Most of the necessary skills are relatively easy to learn. And there are substantial payoffs for managers who learn to select the right employees.

This chapter shows how to avoid common errors in conducting interviews. You will learn to identify the information needed; prepare interview guides; analyze applicants' resumés, applications, and other credentials; conduct thoughtful interviews; and use the information gained to make informed hiring decisions.

What You Need to Know

It is surprising how little some managers know about the people they plan to hire. In fact, many managers seem to go by their feelings. Without being able to say why, many "just know" who they should hire and what the person is worth.

Intuition is an important asset for managers. But research and experience alike show that gut feelings are often wrong, especially when it comes to making hiring decisions. Things may get even more complicated when several managers are involved. One manager likes a particular candidate, a second manager likes another candidate, and the third manager is sure only that the first two are both wrong, dead wrong! The situation can be almost comical when the three try to make a decision. The first manager favors one candidate because he has the best education. The second manager prefers the other candidate because she has the most experience. And the third manager doesn't like either candidate because one won't fit in and the other has a bad attitude. All three points of view are important but the managers may never be able to settle the disagreement. Each has gotten different information from the candidates. In practice, the final decision in these cases is often made in terms that have little to do with the candidates. Either the managers find a way to compromise or the one with the most pull at the moment makes the decision.

There is a better way to make hiring decisions. It starts well before the first ad is posted or the first interview is conducted. The process should always start by taking a careful look at what the employee will be expected to do. What tasks or duties will be assigned to the new employee? How well will he/she have to perform? What standards will be used to evaluate performance?

Answering these questions is more difficult than you may expect, but it is well worth the time. Everything else in the hiring process should follow from a careful analysis of the new employee's job. As a result, the job description should be as specific as possible. Particular tasks and responsibilities should be described as precisely as possible. For example, think about the things you might expect a receptionist to do. In many offices, the receptionist is only required to answer incoming phone calls and greet visitors. Where there are large numbers of incoming calls and frequent visitors, these tasks may occupy several people full-time. In smaller offices, receptionists may also be expected to sort incoming mail, type letters and invoices, maintain a filing system, and fill in when other people are out. The important thing is that there are lots of variations, even with a relatively common position like receptionist. At higher levels and in more technically demanding positions, the variations are even greater.

Identifying tasks and duties provides the foundation for the next step in the process: identifying needed skills and attributes.

When we talk about skills, we mean the ability to do a job correctly. For example, a typist may be required to type eighty words a minute with no more than one error per page. In contrast, attributes refer to the way in which someone goes about doing a job. For example, a secretary may also be required to greet visitors in a friendly manner.

Both skills and attributes are important, but the weight attached to each depends on the nature of the job. Some routine jobs require little interpersonal contact. They may be defined so precisely that we seldom think about the personal attributes required to do them. For example, the skills required by a data entry clerk working alone from detailed instructions are clearly more important than the individual's personal attributes. However, even in this narrowly defined role, some personal attributes are important. It seems reasonable to look for a person who is honest and has enough initiative to seek out answers when unexpected problems arise.

At higher levels and in more complex situations, personal attributes may even be more important than skills. One major retailer rates friendliness as more important than technical skills. "We can always teach someone to run a cash register," they say, "but we haven't yet figured out a way to teach a hostile person to deal with customers the way we like." There are many other cases in which personal attributes are important. Some of the personal attributes frequently mentioned in help-wanted ads are listed in Figure 1.1. We could add many more items to the list. The important point to remember is that personal attributes may be just as important as—and maybe even more important than—the skills required to do a job.

Unfortunately, many interviewers are not skilled judges of personal attributes. That is a big part of the reason that interviews are so unreliable.

Deciding what skills and attributes a person needs to perform the job should also alert you to potential legal complications. Equal opportunity is an important concept in our society and it is the basis

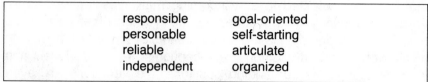

responsible	goal-oriented
personable	self-starting
reliable	articulate
independent	organized

Figure 1.1.   Personal attributes in help-wanted ads

of many laws and regulations affecting employment opportunities. Legislation, executive orders, and judicial precedents have created a body of regulations designed to ensure that employee selection procedures are not disadvantageous to groups that have suffered from discrimination. The Civil Rights Act of 1964, as amended by the Equal Employment Opportunity Act of 1972, is the most frequently cited regulation. Title VII of this act spells out expectations governing all aspects of the selection process.

It shall be unlawful employment practice for an employer—
(1) to fail or to refuse to hire or to discharge any individual or otherwise to discriminate against any individual with respect to his compensation, terms, conditions, or privileges of employment, because of such individual's race, color, religion, sex, or national origin; or
(2) to limit, segregate, or classify his employees or applicants for employment in any way which would deprive or tend to deprive any individual of employment opportunities or otherwise adversely affect his status as an employee, because of such individual's race, color, religion, sex, or national origin.

In layperson's terms, this means that you should not base hiring decisions on factors unrelated to an applicant's ability to do the job. The best way to avoid trouble is to begin by creating a clear and specific list of skills and attributes a person needs to do the job.

So far we have concentrated on job applicants' skills and attributes. There is one more category of information you need to explore: candidates' expectations.

Candidates' expectations are important because they tell you a lot about your chances of hiring each person. They also provide valuable information about how happy the person will be in the job. Suppose you are searching for a receptionist to work forty hours a week (roughly 8 A.M. to 5 P.M. with one hour for lunch). And suppose that you can only afford to pay the person $14,000 per year. That's $7 per hour with two weeks of vacation per year. Under these conditions, it doesn't make sense to spend much time negotiating with applicants who expect a minimum of $10 per hour. And, even if you could hire someone for less than the applicant expects to make, it probably wouldn't be much of a bargain. The person might well resent you and the job, and stay only until something better can be found.

Salary is only one of the expectations you should explore. Other concerns include benefits, working conditions, hours, flexibility, amount of supervision, amount of effort, and opportunities for advancement. These items are important to most applicants, and you should be sure you know what the person expects in each area.

In summary, whenever you prepare to hire someone, you should be prepared to discuss the person's skills, personal attributes, and expectations.

Preparing an Interview Guide

An interview guide is a plan for conducting each interview. The purpose of the guide is to make sure that you ask the right questions, treat each applicant in more or less the same way, and keep a careful record of each interviewee's answers. In practice, an interview guide is a lot like an outline you might use for a speech or presentation.

Like an outline, the interview guide should have a clearly defined introduction, body, and conclusion. And, like an outline, the interview guide should be flexible enough for you to adapt to unexpected circumstances.

The interview guide differs from an outline in one important respect. It provides space to record interviewees' answers. Some skilled managers like to have one sheet for questions and a second sheet to record answers. Other skilled interviewers use a single sheet, with questions in one column and space to record answers in a second column. Both approaches seem to work well, but I prefer the second because there is less chance of materials getting separated or lost.

Figure 1.2 shows a sample interview guide.

Introduction

Greeting

Good morning, John. I'm glad you could join us today. I hope your trip up was easy.

Introduction to Company

We're a small company and you may not have seen much about us in the papers. We were founded just five years ago with only seven employees. Today we have over five hundred employees in four production areas. Our primary products are industrial bearings, precision hydraulic fittings, custom plumbing fixtures, and trophy parts. Most of our customers are located within 750 miles of the plant but we have a few contracts on the West Coast.

Summary of Job

While we have been growing, we haven't had many chances to review our personnel operations. Over the last year it has become clear that we need someone to oversee all of the hiring operations including preparation of job descriptions, advertising, initial screening, and affirmative action reporting. The job you have applied for is a brand new position and we expect the person we hire to move right in and take over.

Body

Why don't you start by telling me a little about your background?

What approach do you use in preparing position descriptions?

What kind of advertising do you prefer? Why?

How do you screen candidates for executive positions?

How many employees did you supervise in your last job?

[Additional questions would be included in a complete interview guide.]

Conclusion

Transition

John, I think you have answered most of my questions. Is there anything you would like to add?

Hiring Process

Let me tell you what's going to happen next. You are the first of seven candidates we will interview for this position. We plan to finish the interviews by the end of next week, and I will probably be able to let you know where we stand by the end of the following week. In the meantime, please be sure to send me copies of the reference letters you mentioned. Thank you for coming out to see me.

Figure 1.2. Sample interview guide

The introduction should be relatively simple and short. Some successful managers say they never bother to plan the introduction—they just wing it—but I don't recommend that approach. The introduction sets the tone for the entire interview, and even casual misstatements can color the entire interview.

Introductions should include three elements. The first is a friendly greeting. Welcoming the candidate just as you would a casual acquaintance may help them feel at ease and increase your chances of getting reliable information. A few questions about topics of common interest will often help the applicant open up, and skilled interviewers are usually prepared to talk about sports, the weather, or current events.

The second element of the introduction should be a *brief* introduction to the company. I emphasize "brief" because you really don't want to overwhelm the applicant. Well-prepared applicants may have already done some background reading, and all you need to do is refresh their memories.

The final part of the introduction is a brief summary of the job. You have to be careful here because you want to explain the kind of work the person will be expected to do without giving them so much information that they will be able to pick the "right" answers even if they aren't qualified.

The body of the interview guide consists of the questions you plan to ask. This should be the longest part of the interview and roughly three-quarters of the interview should be in the body.

There is another important feature of the body you should recognize. Plan to do far less talking than the interviewee during this part of the interview. Precise numbers are arbitrary but you should plan to do less than a quarter of the talking. This gives the interviewee plenty of opportunities to furnish information. It also reduces the danger of feeding too much information to the interviewee. This feature is in marked contrast to the other parts of the interview. You should be prepared to carry the load during both introduction and conclusion, while creating opportunities for the interviewee to speak is a primary task of the body.

While the introduction sets the stage, the body is where you get down to business. This is where you explore the applicant's skills, attributes, and expectations.

Questions are your primary tool. Composing them is not difficult, but some managers prefer to rely on lists of stock questions. The

Table 1.1 Common Interview Questions

Why did you choose your major field of study?

What did you like most about your major?

What did you like least?

How did you get your last job?

What did you like most about your last job?

What did you like least about your last job?

Why did you leave your last job?

What are your long-term goals?

What are your short-term goals?

How will this job contribute to your long-term and short-term goals?

How have your goals changed in the last five years?

Tell me about yourself.

What are your three biggest accomplishments?

What are your three biggest weaknesses?

questions in Table 1.1 are typical of those listed in many interviewing handbooks.

Using stock questions is an easy way to get started. In addition, using current lists of stock questions helps to make sure that you will not accidentally ask illegal or inappropriate questions. However, stock questions are a lot like generic groceries. They meet minimum standards but never really match users' needs and tastes. In the same way, stock questions provide a starting point but never really capture the richness or detail needed to make informed hiring decisions.

Because stock questions are necessarily limited, many skilled managers prefer to compose their own.

There are two sources of direction when you begin writing questions. The first comes from reviewing the credentials submitted by applicants. We will discuss that source in the next section of this chapter.

The second source of direction is the job description. Review the description and make a list of the knowledge, skills, and attributes a person needs to do the job well. Then write appropriate questions.

Working from the list of skills and attributes, you can compose questions designed to see which applicant best fits your needs. Understanding the basic form of some common questions will help you here, as it will in writing questions based on applicants' credentials.

Theorists have developed several ways of classifying questions. Two are most important for our current discussion.

First, some questions are open-ended and call for relatively long answers. Other questions are closed and call for relatively brief answers. Some even ask for one-word answers: "yes" or "no," "more" or "less," and so forth.

Open-ended questions usually get the most information from each applicant. The only problem is that it may be difficult to compare different applicants' answers. For example, "Tell me about yourself" is a favorite of many recruiters. As you can see, this is a very open-ended question. It calls for a long answer, and some job applicants can talk for hours on this subject. Unfortunately, one applicant may emphasize education, while another may describe work experience, and a third may discuss professional expectations. In contrast, "Did you graduate from college?" is a closed question (some experts call it a bipolar question) and most people will answer "yes" or "no." A few people will add qualifications ("No, but I went to Smith University for three years"), but it is still easy to compare their answers.

The distinction between open and closed questions is important because each type is suited to getting certain kinds of information. Closed questions work best for getting information about a person's knowledge and skills, while open questions are best for getting information about a person's attributes and expectations.

We'll look at some more examples in a page or two, but first we should look at the second way of classifying questions. Some questions ask for the specific piece of information the interviewer wants. These are known as direct questions because they ask for the information directly. For example, "Where did you go to college?" and "What was your major?" are commonly used as direct questions.

Direct questions are used more often than the alternative because they are relatively simple to compose and there is little danger of misinterpreting answers. Unfortunately, you can't always expect interviewees to answer honestly. Sometimes social conventions distort answers. For example, some people will not talk openly about their health, weight, income, age, or other personal information. In other cases, self-interest gets in the way. Few interviewees will say "no" when asked if they are reliable. Finally, there are some cases where an interviewee may not be able to answer accurately because they don't share your frame of reference. When someone says they are hardworking you don't know what their standard is or to whom they are comparing themselves.

Social conventions, self-interest, and different frames of reference make it difficult to discuss some topics directly. Indirect questions may give you the best chance of getting reliable information in these situations.

The difference between direct and indirect questions is subtle but important. Whereas direct questions ask for the specific piece of information the interviewer wants, indirect questions ask for related information that will let the interviewer draw an inference—make an educated guess about—the desired data. Let's look at a couple of examples.

"What would you do if you were walking down the street and saw the person in front of you accidentally drop a $50 bill?" This is a direct question if the interviewer really wants to know what you would do in that specific situation. However, it is an indirect question if the interviewer is trying to find out how honest you are.

Another example: "What are your three greatest weaknesses?" This is a direct question if the interviewer really wants to know what you think your weaknesses are. However, it is an indirect question if the interviewer really wants to know if you are mature enough to reveal your perceived weaknesses or how you respond under pressure.

The difference between direct and indirect questions is important because there are times you will need to use indirect questions to get honest answers. This is often the case when exploring personal attributes and it may also arise when discussing applicant expectations. Applicants with little full-time work experience may not have an adequate frame of reference to talk about their expectations, and you may use indirect questions to get a sense of what they really want. You may also use indirect questions to explore knowledge and skills if you doubt an interviewee's honesty.

Analyzing Applicants' Credentials

The second step in the hiring process is reviewing the credentials submitted by job applicants. "Credentials" is a general term that refers to all materials submitted by job seekers. Credentials usually include letters of application, resumés, and written applications. In some cases credentials also include letters of recommendation, work histories, including evaluations of prior supervisors, and samples of work completed.

Reviewing applicants' credentials is important because they often show how well each applicant is prepared for the particular position. Careful review of the credentials may also suggest possible problems that you should explore in the interview. Both the form and the content of the credentials are important. The following paragraphs illustrate some of the more common features that you may want to examine.

Begin by reviewing the overall appearance of the applicant's credentials. Look at the materials as if you were reviewing items a friend planned to submit. Applicants' credentials are—or should be—their best efforts to create a favorable impression. Errors suggest carelessness and inattention to detail that may limit the applicant's value. At the very least, errors indicate that greater than usual effort will be required to train the applicant and raise performance to a professional level.

As you review the credentials, keep a professional standard in mind. Cover letters and resumés should be neatly typed or typeset, easy to follow, and free of errors in spelling, grammar, and format. Application forms and other materials completed while waiting for the interview should be easy to read, generally neatly printed in ink.

As you are reviewing the credentials, note any blanks or omissions. Well-designed application forms are relatively easy to review because blanks stand out. Resumés may be a little more difficult to survey but look for the essentials: education and work history. Look also for basic information you will need to contact the applicant—for example, address and phone number.

Missing information does not mean that you should be reluctant to interview the applicant, but it does mean that you will need to ask some additional questions. Many successful interviewers make a list of missing information and begin each interview by reviewing the applicant's credentials and filling in the blanks.

After noting missing information, carefully examine the applicant's education. Education may not be the most important item in making a hiring decision, but it doesn't make sense to spend time with someone who has not completed minimum requirements. Check to see that appropriate schools, degrees, and classes are listed. Has the person completed the necessary courses and received necessary certification? Are grades, outside activities, and personal interests consistent with the demands of the job? Here again, note any inconsistencies and be prepared to ask about them during the interview.

Work history is the next item to review. Make sure that you know what each job title means and look to see if the listed responsibilities are consistent with the title. If you don't know what the titles mean or if they don't match the listed responsibilities, make a note to ask for clarification. Then look to see if there are any gaps or periods of time during which the person has not listed employment. Professionals may experience periods of unemployment while looking for work or returning to school, but frequent and unexplained gaps may disguise problems. These problems can be just below the surface, just waiting for you to explore. Applicants will frequently forget to mention jobs from which they were fired or laid off after relatively short periods. Medical and other problems may also give rise to periods of unemployment. Again, the presence of gaps does not mean that you should not interview the person, but they do point to topics that should be explored in the interview.

While reviewing the work history, you should also look for three red flags—signs of potential trouble. The first flag is frequent and unexplained job changes. In some fields a person is expected to move every few years, while frequent movement is uncommon in other areas. Ask yourself if the person's history is consistent with the general pattern in the field. Someone who moves too often may be moving to escape problems. Someone who stays in each job longer than expected may have little ambition and may have difficulty coping with change.

The second flag involves the person's reason for leaving a job. In our society we expect people to change jobs for higher salaries. Movement to a lower paying, less responsible job raises a red flag that should be explored. Leaving a job for personal reasons may also disguise problems that need to be explored. One of the easiest ways of exploring potential problems in this area is to ask the interviewee for more detail. You should also see if the applicant will provide the names of two or more references for their time at each past employer.

The final element of the work history to explore is the progression from one job to the next. Is there a clear line of development as a person moves from one job to the next? Do the changes reflect growing skills and knowledge or do they appear random and undirected? A clear pattern of growing skill and responsibility is characteristic of most professionals. Departures from the pattern should be explored because they may be signs of trouble.

This is also a good time to look at the applicant's stated career goal or objective. Most application forms leave out career goals and some resumé forms do not use them. This is unfortunate because each applicant's goal provides a context for many other items of information. For example, you can expect the applicant's work history to show development toward the objective. Similarly, the job for which the person has applied should be part of a developing package of skills, abilities, and experiences pointing toward the long-term objective. (If the applicant has not stated a long-term goal, be sure to ask.) If either the work history or the position for which the person has applied are not logical parts of the progression, you should be sure to question the applicant's goals and objectives during the interview.

You may also look at any preferences and expectations listed by applicants. Are they willing to travel or relocate if necessary? Are there areas or countries where they prefer not to work? Is their salary history consistent with the position for which they have applied? Have they set any other limits on their availability?

Finally, review each applicant's credentials for any inconsistencies. Overlaps in time may point to areas to explore. For example, someone going to school in New York in 1986 may also have had a job in California during the same year, but you ought to explore the relationship between the two activities. In addition, look to see if the person's education matches his or her experiences. Education may also be the source of any special skills or abilities. Similarly, look at the relationship between the applicants' references, on the one hand, and his or her education and employment history, on the other. The value of references that are not clearly related to either education or work should be questioned. Finally, jobs or training programs that do not produce references may raise red flags.

The checklist in Figure 1.3 is based on the categories discussed above. You should review each applicant's credentials before interviewing the person. This checklist is a convenient means of noting areas for exploration.

What materials are included in the credentials?

_____ cover letter

_____ resumé

_____ academic transcripts(s)

_____ letters of recommendation

_____ samples of written or other work

What is the overall appearance of the credentials?
Are they neat and easy to read?
Are they properly formatted?
Are they free of errors in spelling and grammar?

Does the resumé include all necessary information?

_____ educational background

_____ work history

_____ current address

_____ phone number(s)

_____ names of three or more references

_____ special skills or aptitudes

Is the applicant's education consistent with the job for which he or she has applied?

_____ academic degrees

_____ professional certification

_____ grades

_____ activities

_____ personal interests

Is the work history consistent with the job for which he or she has applied?
Do duties and tasks match?
Is the salary history consistent with duties and tasks?
Are there unexplained gaps or periods of unemployment?
Does the work history show continuous growth and development?
Are reasons for leaving clearly stated and consistent with a pattern of growth and development?

Are the applicant's expectations spelled out?
Is the career goal clearly stated?
Is the applicant willing to relocate?
Is the applicant willing to travel?

Are there any inconsistencies?
Do references match education and work history?
Are sources of special skills identified?

Figure 1.3. Credential review checklist

Conducting Thoughtful Interviews

By following the suggestions above, you have already done a great deal of preparation for the interviews. Working in the order suggested, you have identified the skills and attributes a person needs to do the job, prepared questions, composed an interview guide, and reviewed credentials.

As you will soon see, this work has not been wasted. In fact, by this point you are so well prepared that the actual interviews will be a breeze. Most people find the experience far more pleasant than they had imagined possible.

With the work you have already done, you really hav ` a script to guide you through each interview. The hard work has already been done, and you can greet each candidate with confidence because you know in advance what you need to accomplish in each interview. Of course there will be some variation from interview to interview; each candidate is unique, so you want to respond to each as an individual. However, your basic plan will allow you to concentrate on the individual because you won't be preoccupied about what to say or ask.

Common sense is a reliable guide to much of what you do now. You can choose communication styles that match the structure of the interview. An analytic style works best in the introduction and conclusion since you are expected to carry the load. A behavioral style should predominate in the body, but you may need to slip into a consultative style occasionally.

To make sure the interviews go well, set aside enough time. In general, you can probably conduct a reasonably thorough interview in 30 to 45 minutes. Blocking out an hour insures that you will have adequate time and can set both you and the interviewee at ease.

At the same time, be sure to create an appropriate climate. Select a private, professional location and ask your secretary to hold all routine calls. You may be interrupted for emergency calls but, with any luck, there won't be many in the course of an interview. In the worst possible case, if you are distracted by a major emergency you probably owe it to yourself and to the candidate to reschedule the interview.

Having set aside time and chosen an appropriate location, you can begin the interview by simply launching into your script. Begin with a warm, professional greeting and move through your planned introduction. Before moving into the body, you may want to ask about loose ends you found in the credentials. Or you may choose to raise those questions as you discuss the appropriate areas in the body. If that seems too easy, remember that the work you have already done makes it possible for you to concentrate instead on the sole remaining barrier to conducting thoughtful interviews: getting the interviewee to answer your questions.

If you ever have a chance to listen to someone else conduct an interview, or if you carefully read interview transcripts, you will notice that many questions are never satisfactorily answered. There are three things that may happen to prevent a complete or adequate answer.

Sometimes interviewees give incomplete or partial answers. For example, interviewees may respond to the question "Tell me about your education" by describing only their most recent studies and overlooking other potentially relevant experiences.

In other cases, interviewees may get sidetracked; they start to answer a question but allow themselves to get distracted along the way. For example, an interviewee may start describing their educational background, mention that they played football in college, and wind up talking about a team-mate they saw on television the night before.

Finally, some interviewees say things that are simply inconsistent. For example, I once heard an interviewee say that he attended college for four years on an academic scholarship but failed to graduate because his grades fell off in the final semester. That might be possible under unusual circumstances—if the student failed a required course—but it doesn't seem likely that a student who maintained a grade point average good enough to hold a scholarship for four years would fail to graduate just because of poor grades in one semester.

These three kinds of problems—incomplete answers, digressions, and inconsistent answers—all need to be explored in the course of an interview. Unfortunately, many interviewers fail to recognize the problems when they arise. A smaller number of interviewers recognize the problems but don't have the tools they need to explore the answers further.

However, you can avoid these difficulties if you have prepared a complete interview guide—you can concentrate on the interviewee's answers because you don't have to think about what you need to ask next—but it also helps to know how to probe for additional details.

Interview probes are conversational devices that make it possible to get additional details, redirect answers, and explore contradictions. Although we could probably list many more, there are eight specific kinds of probes that will help you deal with most of the situations you will encounter.

The first kind of probe is *silent attention*. Silence is a powerful way of telling the other person to keep talking; it is surprising to see how much some people will reveal about themselves if you give them a chance. Some interviewers make the mistake of concentrating so narrowly on the questions they want to ask that they never really give the interviewees a chance to express themselves fully. As a handy rule of thumb, plan to allow five to eight seconds of silence at the end of each statement by an interviewee. This gives them time to complete their answers and add details.

Mirror statements are the second kind of probe you may want to use. Mirror statements are also called reflective statements because they mirror or reflect back a word or phrase used by the interviewee. They have the effect of saying, "That's interesting, I'd like to hear more." The following examples show how effective they can be when used properly.

INTERVIEWER: Please tell me about your education.

INTERVIEWEE: I attended LMT for two years and then transferred to CST when I was awarded a scholarship.

INTERVIEWER: Scholarship.

INTERVIEWEE: Yes, it was an academic scholarship based on my grades for the first two years. It provided enough support for me to give up my part-time job and concentrate on school.

INTERVIEWER: Part-time job.

INTERVIEWEE: Oh, didn't I mention it? I was working between twenty and thirty hours a week while going to school at LMT.

Neutral phrases also show interviewees that you are interested in what they are saying and ask them to keep going. "Yes," "uhm-hum,"

"OK," "I see," and "that's interesting" are all brief phrases that you can interject to show your interest without breaking the interviewee's train of thought. The following sketch shows an interviewer using several neutral phrases to encourage an interviewee to keep talking.

INTERVIEWER: I see you worked for Skopec Associates while in Long Beach.

INTERVIEWEE: Yes. I did some of their accounting and then had a chance to meet several of their clients.

INTERVIEWER: I see.

INTERVIEWEE: Most of their clients had small businesses of their own, and the job gave me a chance to meet quite a few people. They let me do a little consulting on my own.

INTERVIEWER: That's interesting.

INTERVIEWEE: In fact, I developed three major projects while I was there.

Internal summaries are used to collect an interviewee's remarks about a topic of interest. They pull together things the interviewee may have said at several different points in an interview. They ensure that you remember everything that is relevant and have interpreted it correctly. They also give the interviewee a chance to catch any inconsistencies or correct any misstatements. The following example shows a skilled interviewer summarizing what the interviewee said about her work experience.

Let me make sure I have everything down here. I understand that you went to work as a waitress when you finished high school and continued working at the same restaurant while you went to college. After graduation you worked as a hostess for a few months while looking for a full-time job in advertising. You began with the Bartles-Thom agency and moved to the Smith-Horton agency after five years. You have been with them seven years and are now looking for a chance to move into management. Have I left anything out?

Elaboration is a little stronger way to get an interviewee to continue talking about a particular subject. The interviewer takes the word or phrase that comes closest to the subject in need of discussion and asks the interviewee to say more on the topic. This is particularly useful if the interviewee has gotten distracted and you want to get back to the topic. The following example shows a skilled manager dealing with an applicant who keeps getting sidetracked.

INTERVIEWEE: I developed three major projects while working for them. Then I got a chance to go back to school and . . .

INTERVIEWER: [interrupting gently] Can you tell me a little more about those projects?

INTERVIEWEE: Sure. The first involved landscaping for a small hotel. It was an old hotel that had just reopened. The owner was a real nice guy and he had some real neat ideas.

INTERVIEWER: I'd like to hear more about your role in the landscaping.

Clarification is also a powerful device for getting interviewees back on track. While elaboration asks an interviewee to say more about a particular topic, clarification focuses on the interviewer's question. The following examples are typical.

INTERVIEWER: What was it like working for RDD?

INTERVIEWEE: I spent a lot of time on the phones and I also had a chance to meet several clients.

INTERVIEWER: When I asked what it was like, I wanted to know how you felt about the work.

INTERVIEWER: How often did you meet customers?

INTERVIEWEE: Oh, almost every day.

INTERVIEWER: How often did you meet each one?

Repetition is the seventh form of probe. It can be used whenever an interviewee misses the point of a question, either because they got distracted or didn't seem to hear the question in the first place.

INTERVIEWER: When could you start working for us?

INTERVIEWEE: I really enjoy starting early in the morning.

INTERVIEWER: When could you start working for us?

INTERVIEWER: How many classes do you need to complete your degree?

INTERVIEWEE: Not many, just a few hours.

INTERVIEWER: How many classes do you need to complete your degree?

The final form of probe we will look at is *confrontation*. I list it last because it is an extremely powerful device but may create an awkward situation if it is not used with great care. Confrontation takes two things an interviewee said about a subject, points to a contradiction or inconsistency, and asks the interviewee to explain the apparent disagreement.

INTERVIEWER: Your resumé makes it look like you have already graduated but you say that you need a few more classes. What's up?

INTERVIEWER: You say that you managed three projects but you have only talked about two. Why?

As you can see, confrontations are powerful tools. They can also be dangerous because you may sound like you are picking a fight. Nevertheless, they are invaluable when used with care and respect.

These eight probes are powerful devices to make sure you get the information you need from applicants. We have shown you some examples of each, and the transcript reproduced in the Karen Smith case following this chapter shows some more. They are relatively easy to use, but they are truly valuable only when you listen carefully to the answers you receive.

Making the Selection

By the time you have conducted a series of interviews, you will probably find candidates clustered into three groups. The first or "A" group includes all of the people you really want to hire. These are the people with all the necessary skills and attributes and whose expectations match the working conditions. With luck there will be two or three but probably not more than five.

The second group consists of your "B" candidates. These are applicants who could do the job. They have most of the needed skills and attributes, and their expectations are close enough to yours that you don't anticipate real problems. However, you still have specific reasons for preferring the A group. Although they are in second place, applicants in this group are important because you may need to hire one or more of them if none of your A choices are available.

The final group is your "C" group. These are the applicants you simply will not hire, even if neither the As nor Bs are available. Remember, you need to have concrete, job-related reasons for placing people in this group. You cannot base your decision on race, color, religion, sex, or national origin. In addition, you cannot base your decision on age if the applicant is legally employable.

Once you have divided applicants into three categories, do a reference check on each of the A candidates. There is always the danger that the materials submitted to you have been deliberately falsified. Some candidates also give deceptive answers to questions, so you need to verify the candidates' credentials.

Phone calls are the conventional means of conducting reference checks. They are fast and convenient, and you may be able to conduct several in an hour. Before calling, make a list of the things you need to verify. These usually include the applicant's dates of employment, job titles, responsibilities, perceived performance, and—when appropriate—reason for leaving.

Some employers will freely give a great deal of information while others will only verify that someone worked for a specific period of time. Regardless of the employer's preference, you have a good chance of getting the information you need if you use the following procedure.

Begin by introducing yourself. Your introduction should be cordial but brief and businesslike.

Good morning, Mr. Smith. My name is Alex Johnson. I'm the production manager at LMV Corporation in Long Beach.

Next, explain your reason for calling. Again, plan to be brief and to the point.

> One of your employees, Stuart Jones, has applied for a job with us. I am calling to verify his credentials.

Pause here to let the other person respond. Most people will begin summarizing their experience with the candidate if they can talk freely. Other people are limited by their feelings or by company policy. They will usually signal reluctance to talk by explaining their company policy or by asking for information about the job. When you encounter this response, be prepared to describe the job for which the person has applied. The description you prepared for interviews with the candidates will usually provide sufficient information. You should also be prepared to summarize elements of the candidate's experience that you would like to verify. Although this summary may not be necessary, it often helps the other person start talking. The following summary would usually be enough.

> According to Stuart, he started working for you as a part-time clerk in 1982 while going to school. I understand that he has worked for you ever since and is now your shipping manager.

Again, this is a good point to pause and let the other person talk.

Most references will talk freely, so you should be prepared to take notes. Others will need a bit of prodding, and you can use the probes you learned earlier to solicit the needed information. Use the list of "points to verify" as a checklist to make sure the reference has covered the points you think are important. You may also need to ask a few direct questions, but the checklist will guide you to them as needed.

After you have gotten the information you need and the reference has begun to run down, it is time to conclude the call.

Professional recruiters often close with one of two questions designed to pick up any loose ends.

> Is there anything else you would like to tell me about Stuart?

> Is there anything else I should know about Stuart?

Once your final question has been answered, thank the other person and conclude the call. Occasionally you may want to leave your phone number so the reference can call you back with additional information. This is not necessary and it may not be appropriate in some situations.

Your notes from the reference check should be added to the candidate's file to form a complete package. Many recruiters make it a practice to check two or three references for each candidate. They know that references sometimes have their own motives. Some have personal axes to grind. Others say negative things about employees they would like to keep and good things about employees they want to leave. Checking with more than one reduces chances of forming an inappropriate opinion.

Once you have finished checking credentials, you are ready to make your decision. Checking references may reduce your "A" list to one or two candidates. This is natural as you learn more about each candidate. If you are lucky, one candidate will be so clearly superior that the choice is easy. Even if there are two or more superior candidates, you have enough information to make a reasoned decision. This is where your professional judgment counts. Having screened all of the candidates and checked references for those on your A list, you probably can't go wrong by much, even if your intuition misleads you. Pick the most promising candidate and be comfortable with the fact that you have done everything within reason to make the best possible choice.

Conclusion

This chapter began by looking at the kind of problems that result when selection decisions are not made with care. You have seen that managers at all levels are becoming more and more involved in selection decisions and you have been introduced to skills needed to avoid some common errors.

You are now prepared to conduct interviews by reviewing the demands of the position, preparing an interview guide, analyzing applicants' credentials, conducting thoughtful interviews, and making a reasoned selection after checking credentials.

The Karen Smith case following this chapter is designed to help you develop your skills further. It contains a sample position description, some typical credentials, and an interview transcript.

Suggested Readings

Avery, Richard D., and James E. Campion. "The Employment Interview: A Summary of Recent Research." *Personnel Psychology* 35 (1982): 281–322.

Cascio, Wayne F. *Applied Psychology in Personnel Management.* 2d ed. Reston, Virginia: Reston Publishing, 1982.

Deal, Terrence E., and Allan A. Kennedy. *Corporate Cultures.* Reading, Massachusetts: Addison-Wesley Publishing Company, 1982.

Einhorn, Lois J., Patricia Hayes Bradley, and John E. Baird, Jr. *Effective Employment Interviewing.* Glenview, Illinois: Scott, Foresman and Company, 1982.

Mandel, Jerry E. "A Strategy for Selecting and Phrasing Questions in an Interview." *Journal of Business Communication* 12 (1974): 17–23.

Reilly, Richard R., and Georgia T. Chao. "Validity and Fairness of Some Alternative Employee Selection Procedures." *Personnel Psychology* 34 (1982): 1–62.

Schmenner, R. W., "How Can Service Businesses Survive and Prosper?" *Sloan Management Review* 27 (1986): 21–32.

Skopec, Eric William. *Situational Interviewing.* Prospect Heights, Illinois: Waveland Press, 1988.

Wallach, Ellen J. "Individuals and Organizations: The Cultural Match." *Training & Development Journal* (February 1983): 23–36.

Zima, Joseph P. *Interviewing: Key to Effective Management.* Chicago: Science Research Associates, 1983.

Case Study:
Diana Jones

Diana sat slumped at her desk. The last hour and a half had not been pleasant. For the first time in her managerial career she had had to fire an employee, but she still didn't know what had gone wrong. The following pages display the information on which she based her original hiring decision.

POSITION DESCRIPTION: Senior technical inspector; duties include sampling production runs, checking samples for consistency, identifying and reporting defects, supervising three junior technical inspectors, and managing the technical lab budget.

Chad Smith
8107 Brockport Lane
Newton, California

OBJECTIVE: A senior technical quality control
                    position providing security and a
                    chance for advancement.

EDUCATION: B.S., Physics, New University
                    Oldtown, Kentucky, 1985

                    M.B.A., New University
                    Old Town, Kentucky, 1986

WORK HISTORY: 1985—present, Teacher
                    Mark Morris High School
                    Los Angeles, California

                    1982—1985   Lab Supervisor
                    Student Chemistry Lab
                    New University, Oldtown, Kentucky

                    1980—1983   Salesman and Assistant
                    Manager
                    Smith Brothers' Mens' Clothing
                    Newton, California

PERSONAL DATA: I am in good health and enjoy travel.
                    I am willing to relocate anywhere in
                    California.

August 5, 1987
To whom it may concern:

Chad Smith has worked as a Salesman and Assistant
Manager in my clothing store for the past five years. He
has shown himself to be intelligent, industrious, and
courteous. He was extraordinarily popular and several
regular customers still ask about him whenever they shop.
I have complete confidence in his ability to grow into a
mature professional in any field he chooses.

Signed,

Chad Smith, senior

Dear Ms. Jones:

Chad Smith has asked me to write this letter in support of his application for a position with you.

I have known Chad for several years. He was a student in my Sociology of Religion Course in 1983 and he is one of the few students who has remained in contact with me. I know him to be courteous, friendly, and popular. He is well regarded by his peers and several of my colleagues have spoken favorably of him.

Chad is at his best in situations working with other people. He is a natural leader and has been active in several societies on campus.

I hope this letter provides the material you need.

Sincerely yours,

C. William Howard
Assistant Professor

DIANA: Why did you choose your major field of study?

CHAD: Most of my friends were picking softer majors—things like political science and sociology. I guess those are OK for some people but I wanted something that would let me make a real contribution, something solid that I knew would pay off in the future.

DIANA: What did you like most about your major?

CHAD: The fact that there is always a right answer. Some subjects are so fuzzy that you never know when you have things right, but in physics you can always tell when you have the right answer.

DIANA: What did you like least?

CHAD: During my senior year, we had to take a course in research methods. That course just about undid everything we had learned—no right answers or procedures, just a bunch of guesses about approaches to problems most people never have to deal with.

DIANA: How did you get your last job?

CHAD: I couldn't find a job in industry so I took a short teacher certification course. When I finished there were so many jobs for teachers that I just sat back and waited for school districts to contact me. The folks in Los Angeles called before anyone else and gave me more money than anyone else.

DIANA: What did you like most about your last job?

CHAD: Grading.

DIANA: What did you like least about your last job?

CHAD: Parent conferences, especially when students were in trouble.

DIANA: Why did you leave your last job?

CHAD: I haven't yet; I'm getting a little bored and I don't like the politics I have to deal with. My contract runs out at the end of this year but I can probably leave earlier if I get a good offer.

DIANA: What are your long-term goals?

CHAD: I really don't know yet. I think I need to get established in an industry before I can make any long-term plans for myself.

DIANA: What are your short-term goals?

CHAD: To get a job outside teaching.

DIANA: Have you taken a course in sampling methods?

CHAD: Yes.

DIANA: Are you familiar with our testing procedures?

CHAD: Yes, Steve who works in your technical lab is a friend of mine and he explained them to me.

DIANA: Have you ever supervised other technicians?

CHAD: Yes; at school I was responsible for student lab projects and I directed a group of seven student technicians.

2

Coaching and Delegation

At one time, managers were evaluated solely for their ability to get something out of their people. Today, the ability to put something back—to help subordinates grow and develop—is just as important. Many senior executives believe that managers are not ready for promotion until they have prepared others to take their places. As a result, successful managers spend much time teaching and coaching.

Delegation is one of the most ancient tasks of management. Although delegation has its roots in classical theories of organization, the process is far more complicated today than it once was. In bygone eras, managers just divided jobs into parts, gave several people a piece of the task, and kept an eye on them. Today's workers want to know why the job is divided the way it is, why they are given a particular piece, and how they will benefit from doing their part. The changing composition of the workforce makes understanding employee motivation more important than at any time in the past.

This chapter will introduce a four-step approach to delegation: selecting a capable subordinate, explaining the task, providing needed resources, and keeping in touch. Each step communicates a manager's expectations; readers will learn how to communicate positive expectations and encourage high levels of performance.

Even today, some managers are surprised by the attention given to delegation and coaching. "Why make all the fuss," they ask, "when all you have to do is tell people what to do and kick ___ if they don't get it done?" Although we may find it objectionable, the attitude underlying the question may have worked well in less challenging circumstances.

When little employee initiative was required and most work took place in carefully controlled production lines, employees were valued—if at all—for their hands, not their heads.

Today, increased competition and the changing nature of work require more. With growing competition, ideas that may give rise to competitive advantages need to be sought at every level. At the same time, most work has evolved to mental work that cannot be counted, measured, and controlled in the same way that assembly line production can be.

As a result, employees' ideas are at least as important as their mechanical skills. Under these circumstances, the grudging obedience produced by the "tell 'em what to do, kick 'em in the ___" approach has limited value. In fact, the approach may actually work against you because bright and thoughtful employees will seek more attractive places to work.

There is another factor leading to newer approaches to delegation. As we look at demographic patterns, it is easy to see that many

Almost two-thirds of the new entrants into the workforce between now and the year 2000 will be women, and 61 percent of all women of working age are expected to have jobs by the year 2000. Women will still be concentrated in jobs that pay less than men's jobs, but they will be rapidly entering many higher-paying professional and technical fields. In response to the continued feminization of work, the convenience industries will boom, with "instant" products and "delivery-to-the-door" service becoming common throughout the economy. Demands for day care and for more time off from work for pregnancy leave and child-rearing duties will certainly increase, as will interest in part-time, flexible, and stay-at-home jobs.
—William B. Johnston and Arnold H. Packer, *Workforce 2000* (Indianapolis, Indiana: Hudson Institute, 1987), p. xx.

companies will face labor shortages in the near future. The problems will be particularly severe in areas calling for skilled, intelligent employees. Worse yet, the quality of high school graduates is reaching all-time lows. Recent studies indicate that only one in five can even read a bus schedule and fewer than one in twenty can compose a simple one-page letter applying for a job.

These changes have already forced many managers to find new ways of delegating work and developing employees. Let's look at the story of one manager who has learned from his experiences.

Learning to Delegate

When he finished business school, Steve Smith took a job as head of the Accounting Department for a new company, ACME Widgets. Calling him head of the department was a bit of a stroke for his ego but didn't mean that he had a great deal of managerial responsibility. There was only one person in the department: Steve Smith.

Work in the department was simple but important. Hour by hour, people brought him records of transactions affecting the company. John made a $50 sale, Maintenance bought $75 worth of rags, Mary charged $20 worth of office supplies, John made another $50 sale, and so on. Hour by hour, day by day, and week by week, Steve received reports of these transactions.

These transactions are the life of the business. But by themselves the individual transaction receipts didn't tell much about the state of the business. Looking at the stack of receipts, no one could tell whether ACME Widgets was making a profit, or even if it could afford to pay its bills! Steve's job, like the job of accounting departments everywhere, was to convert these isolated transaction receipts into meaningful reports: profit-and-loss statements, cash-flow summaries and projections, quarterly and annual reports.

Delegation of responsibility has been a central topic in management texts through the ages. But today's marketplace, which demands heretofore unheard-of front-line freedom to initiate far-reaching actions, propels the subject toward the top of the list.
—Tom Peters, *Thriving on Chaos* (New York: Alfred A. Knopf, 1988), p. 450.

Since ACME was a small company, Steve could handle most of the work by himself. Of course there were a few late nights and a couple of long weekends during his first two years. But he still managed to keep things under control.

Over the next few years, ACME prospered and the work in Steve's area grew by leaps and bounds. Instead of a few late nights, Steve found himself working ten and twelve hours almost every day. And the weeks before quarterly reports were almost impossible: long hours, late nights, lost weekends.

Steve finally reached the breaking point and asked to meet with his boss, Carol Olson, President of ACME. Carol listened to Steve's problems, reviewed the latest budget projections, and agreed that it was time to hire a clerk to help.

Steve turned to the Personnel Department—also a one-person department because ACME was still a small company—and they quickly found several candidates to come in for interviews. Steve had little difficulty picking the best—JoAnn, who had attended the same business school.

Steve wasn't sure how to make the best use of JoAnn. He began by identifying the mechanical or routine parts of his job. He quickly settled into a pattern. He read each transaction receipt and put a note on it telling JoAnn where to record the information, how to file the original receipt, and asking her to report when finished.

Although the procedure was easy to understand, it didn't seem to make Steve's life much easier. He still found himself putting in long hours and giving up his weekends. Steve thought about asking for more help but realized that Carol wouldn't be too enthusiastic about hiring another person so soon.

Steve spent his first free weekend thinking about the problem. He decided that his life would be easier if he spent less time with each transaction receipt. Rather than putting a note on each, he decided to divide them into piles requiring similar actions: one stack for income, one for expenditures, and another for "other" concerns. With everything clustered, Steve could simply put a note on top of each stack so that JoAnn would know what to do.

This new system reduced the amount of time Steve had to spend writing, but he quickly found that it wasn't enough to keep him out of trouble. He still found himself putting in long hours and missing weekends with his family. And he still couldn't keep up with the work generated by ACME's growth.

When the quarter came to an end, Steve worked three straight twenty-hour days—Friday, Saturday, and Sunday—to finish the necessary reports. JoAnn noticed that he was in a bad mood on Monday and made a suggestion she thought might help. "Why don't you let me divide the transactions into piles and record each? I can set aside those I don't understand, and you can check my work to make sure I don't mess up."

"That's a nice idea," Steve said, "but I always read each receipt. Let me think about it and I'll get back to you."

Steve liked JoAnn's idea but he wasn't sure if he trusted her. What would happen, he wondered, if JoAnn made a mistake and recorded an expense as income? That would screw up the whole system and make the reports worse than meaningless. "We just can't afford to take that chance," he told himself, and so he told JoAnn that he appreciated her willingness to help but that the records were just too important to take a chance on a new system.

Things ran pretty much as usual for the next quarter. Steve noticed that his days got longer and longer while JoAnn always seemed to have plenty of time for her work. Even as ACME got more business and the stack on his desk got higher and higher, JoAnn's desk remained clean and orderly. She even had time to take long lunches and to arrange birthday parties for other people in the office.

Getting out the next quarterly report was almost impossible. Steve put in four twenty-hour days and still missed the deadline—for the first time in his career. "Something has to be wrong here," Steve told himself. "JoAnn works for me but she has time for all this other stuff while I'm killing myself just trying to keep up."

As he thought about the situation, Steve was as mad as he had ever been. "Maybe I should fire JoAnn and get someone who will be able to help me," he thought. Fortunately, he took time to cool off and think things through. JoAnn was doing everything he asked, and doing it very well. The system was breaking down because ACME's business was booming and he simply didn't have time to review every transaction receipt and do the other things he was supposed to do. Something had to change, and it didn't look like JoAnn was at fault. In desperation, he called her into his office and said, "I've been thinking about your suggestion. Starting tomorrow, I'm going to route all transaction receipts directly to you. I think you know how to handle them but I'd like you to bring any special cases to me. I'll check your work from time to time, but I trust you to do what needs to be done."

In the weeks following this conversation, Steve noticed some important changes in the office. Work still piled up on his desk from time to time, but it was usually "important stuff"—things that required serious thought rather than routine processing. JoAnn had less time for long lunches and more things were beginning to pile up on her desk. Surprisingly, she actually seemed happier and more interested in her work.

Getting the next quarterly report out was a snap, and JoAnn actually said "thank you" to Steve for letting her help.

Of course there were a few errors, but Steve and JoAnn were able to solve the problems. And they were able to take time to create systems to prevent future errors.

Steve didn't even notice the most important change. In a short period of time, he had worked through three stages that summarize many professional managers' careers. He began by doing everything himself. Then he moved to the second stage: delegating specific tasks while keeping all responsibility and authority. Finally, he had learned to give up some of his authority. This was a big step because it required trusting JoAnn enough to give her responsibility for some of his work. This final stage reflects a mature understanding of the manager's role. Let's see what it looks like in more general, theoretical terms.

The Manager's Role

The transition to management is a tough one for many people. As we saw in the Introduction, most people are promoted to management because they are good at doing something. Usually, that something involves working with things. Whether they are accountants, engineers, or financial analysts, they catch the boss's eye because they are better—somehow "more promising"—than their colleagues. Once promoted into management, they continue along a career path without systematic instruction in what it means to be a manager.

Many skilled managers figure out the manager's role on their own. Others copy the behavior of their own supervisors. Unfortunately, some never get thoughtful guidance.

Much of what we know about the manager's role comes from watching successful managers. Scholars have studied managers in

many fields and carefully noted what they do and say. These successful managers usually talk about their organizations as systems.
They describe their jobs in relation to the system.

When we talk about any organization as a system, we mean
something like the simple organization depicted in Figure 2.1. From
a manager's point of view, a system is a group of people, processes,
and equipment brought together to accomplish something. The
"something" can be anything necessary to keep the organization in
business. Many traditional business functions are handled by systems: purchasing, marketing, sales, and customer service are all
business functions handled by systems.

In most organizations, each department or system has at least
one manager. The manager's role is defined in relationship to the
system. Trainers conducting managerial seminars often help managers look at their roles by asking what would happen if they were hit
by a truck on their way to work the next day. A few managers say
that their departments would keep right on producing without them.
Other managers respond that routine work would continue without
them, but special projects and unusual tasks would halt. Finally,

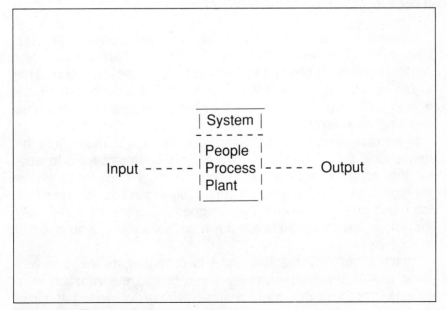

Figure 2.1 The organization as a system

many managers believe that everything would stop, the system could not run without them, and work would simply pile up until someone took over. Take a moment to think which answer you would choose.

If you think about your role as a manager the way many successful managers do, you probably chose the first answer. That is an important choice because it means you have done your work in creating a system and are not required to keep it running.

Successful managers usually pick this answer because they know that their job is creating systems and helping these systems adapt to changes. Managers create adaptive systems by hiring and developing people, securing needed resources, and helping people revise and develop processes.

Of course, there are times when managers need to be involved in the ongoing activities of the system. This is the case when new products (outputs) are being developed, when inputs are changing or unpredictable, when processes are being revised, and when new people are learning their jobs. However, even in these periods, managers should still concentrate on helping the system (the second answer) rather than doing the work themselves (the final answer).

You Can't Get There from Here

We've seen that the manager's job is to develop and refine systems, not to carry out the processes themselves. This is an attractive point of view but it poses a real dilemma for many managers. They are so busy doing the work that they don't have time to train anyone else to do it. How, they ask, can they break the cycle and get someone else involved?

Many managers raise this objection in seminars. They agree that they should be creating systems and getting other people to work, but they argue that while "it's all right in theory it will never work in my organization." These managers usually argue that there is simply too much for them to do. If they stopped doing the work, they say, the whole system would break down because there is no one else to do the job.

That's a serious objection and lots of managers feel that way. What makes the problem really tough is that the situation won't change until these managers change their way of looking at things. As long as they do the work themselves, nobody else is learning how to do it and there is no one else ready to step in and take over. It suggests we need to look a little more closely at the twin processes of delegation and coaching.

Delegation and Coaching Defined

Delegation and coaching are twin processes. Both are vital parts of the manager's job and neither can be done effectively without the other.

Delegating responsibility to other people does not mean abdicating managerial responsibilities for monitoring and supporting the process. Some managers assume an either/or world where either they are in complete control or they have given up all control. But delegation—whether by a management team to a set of employee teams or by a single manager to his or her subordinates—means that the manager not only sets the basic conditions but also stays involved, available, to support employees, reviewing results, redirecting or reorienting the team as necessary.
—Rosabeth Moss Kanter, *The Change Masters* (New York: Simon and Schuster, 1983), p. 250.

In the most general terms, delegation is the process of assigning work to a subordinate. Coaching is the process of helping the subordinate develop the skills and attributes needed to do the job correctly.

To see how these two processes work together, let's look at the steps in the delegation process. The first step is selecting a capable subordinate. By capable, we mean a subordinate who has the needed skills and attributes or who can develop them in time to get the job done.

The second step is explaining the task to the subordinate. This needs to be done in terms that are meaningful to the subordinate—and that is an important qualification. Some subordinates want very specific instructions focusing on each task: do this, do that, and so forth. Other subordinates will chafe at such precise directions. "Just tell me what you want done and let me figure out how to do it" summarizes their attitude. The majority of people fall somewhere between these two extremes.

Giving the subordinate enough authority to do the job is the third step. Relinquishing authority is as difficult for many managers as it was for Steve in the ACME Widget Accounting Department. But giving up authority is absolutely vital. Two things happen when you fail to do so. First, you destroy part of your subordinates' motivation. Before long, they develop a "why should I knock myself out when he doesn't trust me" attitude. Second, when you don't give a subordinate the needed authority, work piles up on your desk—just like it did on Steve's—because you still make all the decisions.

The final step is making arrangements to keep in touch. You may need to meet with young, inexperienced subordinates more often than with older, seasoned employees but both deserve your attention. And both need to know they can come to you when there are problems.

These four steps—selecting a capable subordinate, explaining the task, providing needed authority, and keeping in touch—are the heart of delegation. Coaching should take place at every step in the process. Let's look at the role of coaching at each of these points.

First, in selecting a capable subordinate you need to pick someone who has or can develop the needed skills and attributes. You probably don't have anyone who could do the job as well as you could so there is an immediate opportunity for coaching. Moreover, anyone who could do the job with their eyes closed would probably be bored. You are best advised to pick someone who will learn by doing, and coaching is the best way to make sure that they are learning.

Explaining the task is, first and foremost, coaching. Even at the lowest level, this step involves teaching: teaching how to do the job and why it is done that way. At higher levels, you may concentrate

---

RULES FOR TEACHING
1. Almost everyone enjoys learning; few people enjoy being taught.
2. Adults learn best when they are actively involved in the process.
3. Trust and support promote learning; suspicion and criticism create defensiveness.
4. To be a teacher, you need to see things from the student's point of view.
5. Effective teachers are more than sources of information; they are role models for their students.

less on how-to-do-it and more on what-we're-trying-to-accomplish, but you are still engaged in coaching. The experience of master teachers summarized in the box on page 70 is as important on the job as in the classroom.

Giving the subordinate authority is the next step. The dangerous thing here is that power and authority can go to someone's head very quickly. Few people have much experience and almost all will go wrong when they get started. Learning when to use authority and when to rely on other skills (for example, persuasion) is a vital skill that is seldom taught in school or elsewhere. On the job coaching is the most efficient way to teach, and a central part of any manager's job.

My first job as a manager was a real eye-opener. The job description made it sound like I was a king. I could "order," "instruct," "supervise," and "discipline" all of the people around me. That's a lot of authority but it didn't take the employees long to show me how little power I really had—they went through the motions but nothing got done unless they wanted to do it. I learned that a manager's only real power comes from making sure people want to do what you ask them to do.
—An experienced manager

Making arrangements to keep in touch is the final step. Few subordinates know instinctively how often or when to check with you. Asking for help too often makes them look incompetent, while not asking for help often enough is dangerous because they may get into so much trouble that you will never get things sorted out. The tough thing is that there are no generally accepted definitions of "too often" and "often enough." Subordinates need to develop a feel, an almost intuitive sense of what's right, and coaching is the best way for them to learn.

As you see, delegation and coaching need to work hand in hand. In a way, that's fortunate because both can benefit from use of the same tool—the job expectancy scale.

Job Expectancy Scale

The job expectancy scale is designed to give managers and subordinates a convenient way of discussing delegation. The scale clarifies subordinates' responsibilities for expected day-to-day working relationships.

The amount of responsibility you give to subordinates depends on two things: how much confidence you have in their abilities, and the importance of the job.

When subordinates are new or inexperienced, it makes sense to keep a pretty close eye on their work. This means asking them to report frequently and assuming responsibility for keeping things moving. As subordinates develop, they should assume more responsibility and they should be expected to report less frequently.

The importance of the task is the second factor to consider. Some tasks are so important that you probably want to keep an eye on them, even when assigned to trusted subordinates. Even though the subordinate is competent, the job may simply be so important that close supervision is needed. Other jobs require less time and attention. Some are so minor that they can be entrusted to even relatively inexperienced subordinates.

Deciding how much responsibility to entrust to each subordinate is one of the most important decisions you ever make. Give too little responsibility, and the subordinate will stagnate; give too much responsibility, and failure and frustration may result.

There are six levels of responsibility. Let's start by looking at the highest level and work our way down the scale.

At the highest level, there are some subordinates that can be trusted to do particular tasks without ever reporting. The easiest example is a senior secretary or assistant, who may keep track of administrative details without being required to report on their completion. For example, a senior secretary might be responsible for stocking office supplies, updating client records, and preparing monthly invoices. If the manager has enough faith in the secretary, he or she may instruct the secretary to "just do it; don't worry about keeping me informed." That arrangement has advantages for both the manager and the secretary. It makes it possible for the manager to concentrate on other matters, and it gives the assistant a sense of ownership, encouraging pride and accomplishment.

The second level on the job expectancy scale requires almost as much trust. It differs from the first in asking the subordinate to report at regularly scheduled intervals. For example, the manager may expect a new assistant to maintain supplies, update client records, and prepare monthly invoices, but require him or her to report at regularly scheduled staff meetings.

Like the first, this level shows a great deal of trust in the subordinate. It differs in that the regular reports make it possible for the manager to step in when necessary. The manager may step in when aware of problems emerging that the subordinate has not anticipated. For example, the manager might step in if it is known that a regular supplier will be closing for an extended period and the assistant has not ordered enough material to keep things running until the supplier reopens.

Periodic reports also make it possible for the manager to do additional training. For example, the assistant may not understand the manager's priorities. If the assistant were invoicing the least important clients first, the manager might step in to explain priorities and reorder the subordinate's work.

The third level on the job expectancy scale also permits the subordinate to act but requires a report immediately. Managers may assign this level of responsibility to a subordinate when they want the subordinate to accept responsibility but still feel the need to keep an eye on the process. For example, a manager may expect the assistant to update accounting records, but want to act quickly when mistakes could cause problems for other divisions using the same records. Under these circumstances, it makes sense to give the subordinate full responsibility for the task while requiring him or her to report immediately after all major actions.

The fourth level on the job expectancy scale requires the subordinate to get specific approval *before* acting. At this level, the subordinate may bring something to the manager's attention and suggest an action, but do nothing until the manager gives the OK. For example, some of the client records an assistant maintains may be particularly sensitive. With these records, the assistant may assemble a list of updates but not enter them without the manager's specific approval. Or, even though an assistant is responsible for ordering supplies, the manager might specify the spending limit. The assistant may buy whatever is thought necessary as long as it costs less than $250 per month. Once spending reaches that limit, or if a specific piece of equipment would push spending over the limit, the assistant needs the manager's approval before acting.

The final two levels on the job expectancy scale call for little subordinate initiative. They would normally be used only with subordinates that are very new to the job or with tasks that are extremely sensitive.

At level five, the subordinate asks the manager what to do. Even

Highest level of responsibility	1. act independently, never report
	2. act independently, report routinely
	3. act independently, report immediately
	4. recommend action, do as directed
	5. ask what to do
Lowest level of responsibility	6. wait to be told what to do

Figure 2.2   The job expectancy scale

at this level, the subordinate is expected to recognize the need for action. However, having called a situation to the manager's attention, the subordinate waits for specific instructions before acting.

Level six is the lowest level of responsibility. At this level, the subordinate isn't even expected to recognize the need for action. The subordinate simply waits for the manager to say what to do.

As you can see, levels five and six require relatively little of the subordinate. Nevertheless, they are appropriate starting points. As subordinates grow, they should move up the scale, but levels five and six may still be used for particularly sensitive tasks where the manager wants to be personally involved.

The six levels of the job expectancy scale are summarized in Figure 2.2.

Delegation and Coaching with the Job Expectancy Scale

The job expectancy scale makes it possible to characterize subordinates' responsibilities so clearly that they are never in the dark about their managers' expectations. More important, using the job expectancy scale as part of an ongoing coaching program makes it possible to track each subordinate's progress and to pave the way for their next step.

In most organizations, each subordinate is responsible for several tasks. For example, administrative assistants are frequently responsible for many of the tasks listed in Figure 2.3.

During the first week on the job, most assistants would be expected to act at relatively low levels of initiative on all of these tasks. As they become more familiar with the manager's expecta-

screen incoming calls
produce reports and correspondence
establish and maintain file systems
respond to routine information requests
schedule routine meetings
maintain financial records

Figure 2.3   Administrative assistant's responsibilities

tions, their level of responsibility should grow. For example, Figure 2.4 shows the changing job expectancy levels for an administrative assistant at three points during the first year on the job.

This pattern is a healthy one because it shows a subordinate growing into the job.

By the end of the first year, the subordinate is ready to grow beyond the existing job. This can be accomplished in either of two ways. First, the subordinate can be promoted to a more responsible position—perhaps performing similar duties for a more senior executive. Second, other duties can be added to the list. For example, he or she might be asked to supervise a group of junior assistants or to help design a training program. The important point is that the subordinate should not be allowed to stagnate. Tracking the subordinate's development should be a shared task and both manager and subordinate should keep a record similar to the one shown in Figure 2.4. This makes it possible for both to participate in the subordinate's career planning. And, it makes it possible for both to send up red flags when the subordinate stops growing.

	first week	*first month*	*end of year*
screen incoming calls	5	1	1
produce reports and correspondence	3	3	1
establish and maintain file systems	3	2	1
respond to routine information requests	5	4	3
schedule routine meetings	6	2	2
maintain financial records	6	4	2

Figure 2.4   Growing initiative

Working with Teams

One of the most dramatic changes in many areas of work is the growing use of teams. Rather than assigning work to individual subordinates, today's managers often find themselves delegating projects to groups of people. The groups may range from three or four people to as many as twenty-five or more. Research indicates that groups are most effective with five or seven members, but you may be forced to work with fewer when resources are limited or more when the project is large or many distinct voices want to be heard.

The popular use of teams started as an effort to copy Japanese manufacturing techniques. However, some American managers have always been fond of teams. They like teams because of the advantages of delegating work to a group. Well-coordinated teams can access more talent, information, knowledge, and broader networks than most individuals. At the same time, teams can often solve complex problems faster than individuals, and are more likely to have the political connections to get their suggestions implemented. Finally, teams are less likely to leave a manager stuck out on a limb because other members can carry on even if one is sick, injured, or leaves.

Teams also have limitations. Well-coordinated teams can do wonderful things. Other groups break down into angry clusters, blaming

---

The "small business" mentality that comes from a sociotechnical organization structure is mirrored in the way work is designed. Instead of classifying work into "jobs," the work system in sociotechnical operations is organized so that tasks and jobs become the responsibility of teams of multiskilled people. Teams are responsible for meeting production goals, the way work is organized, safety, housekeeping, training, quality, and often the selection and hiring of new team members. In short, teams take responsibility for a large chunk of the business or process. This "chunking" or team concept approach is spreading rapidly in America: In a 1986 survey of 1,600 companies, the APC [American Productivity Center] found that 8 percent were using self-managed or autonomous teams. Why? It seems to work better than conventional job design.

—C. Jackson Grayson, Jr., and Carla O'Dell, *American Business: A Two-Minute Warning* (New York: The Free Press, 1988), p. 126.

other members of the team when things go wrong while never accepting responsibility for getting things done. Personality conflicts can lead to open feuds, and warring members can antagonize everyone else in the division or company. Worse still, team members may settle on a plan without consulting other members of the organization and then refuse to listen to outside opinions.

As you can see, delegating projects to a team can be a very good strategy. It can also lead to disaster. What makes the difference? Usually the amount of time and effort the manager puts into making the team work effectively as a unit.

No sane manager would assign a major project to a new, inexperienced subordinate without first making sure the project and the procedures to be used were fully understood. Would you? Unfortunately, many managers do just that the first time they try to delegate a project to a team. Taking a group of people with little experience working together or in groups and turning them loose without explaining the project or procedures is asking for trouble. That's what some have done, and most got just what they deserved.

The point to remember is that using teams is not simply good or bad. Teams work well when tasks are delegated to them in an appropriate way. And delegating a task to a group takes just as much or more time than delegating it to an individual.

There is one important difference between delegating work to an individual and delegating it to a team. When you delegate to an individual, your primary concern should be the person's ability to do the job. When you delegate to a group, you may be less concerned about their technical abilities because your primary interest should be the members' ability to work well together. This does not mean that you expect everybody on the team to be friends. It does mean that members need to respect one another and work together in a way that takes advantage of the strengths of each.

Let's look at the delegation process as it applies to teams. The first step is selecting a capable team. When delegating to an individual, you look for someone who has or can develop the needed skills and attributes. Technical skills and knowledge are also important when creating a project team, but no one individual needs to have all of the needed skills or knowledge. All you need to do on this score is assemble a group of individuals who have all the needed skills and knowledge *among* them. In fact, things may not work well if any one individual has all the needed skills and knowledge because that reduces opportunities for other members to contribute.

Far more difficult is selecting people who will work well together. Personality conflicts and feuds can destroy a team, and clever managers usually try to anticipate and avoid them. Speak to each member of the team individually before the group is announced publicly. Explain why you would like the person to participate and how you have chosen the other members. If there are conflicts, deal with them before the team meets as a group.

Group leadership can also create an issue. Some managers prefer to let the group decide. You may even decide that the project is so important that you want to lead the team personally. Whatever you prefer, make sure that each member knows how you made your decision, and that none feels slighted.

Explaining the project is the second step. Most members should have a pretty good idea by the time the group first meets, especially if you've taken the time to talk to each individually. However, there are a couple of procedural points you need to clarify.

Begin by explaining the objective—what you would like the group to accomplish. Are they merely to study a problem and report? Do you expect them to develop recommendations? Or do you want them to make a decision and implement a solution?

The nature of group process is the second point you need to clarify. Why have you decided to turn the project over to a team? Why have you selected this team? Who will be the leader? How will the group make decisions? What procedures should they use? When do you expect them to finish?

Explaining the team objective and describing the procedures will help the group avoid aimless wandering. At the same time, you need to allow the group quite a bit of freedom. If you define the project and procedures so narrowly that the team has few options, the members may feel like a bunch of gofers. When that happens, you lose many advantages of teams and you destroy much of the participants' motivation.

One useful strategy is to summarize your expectations on a flip chart and ask the members to edit your work. Each member should have an opportunity to make changes and corrections so that the team *as a whole* feels that it helped to define the project and procedures.

Providing needed authority is the third step in delegation. You have already begun this process by explaining your objective to the group. The differences between various objectives—study and report, develop recommendations, and decide and implement—reflect fundamental differences in the group's authority.

You may choose to develop teams just as you would individual subordinates. Relatively immature groups should have less authority than mature and sophisticated teams. The word "mature" has a special meaning in this context and you should be sure not to confuse it with age. A mature team is one that has developed the working relationships described in the box on this page. It takes care and skill to develop mature teams. Some groups never become mature, no matter how long they work together. Other groups become mature very quickly because they are guided by skilled facilitators.

Teams are mature when their members (1) are committed to a common goal, (2) understand and accept procedures used to make decisions, and (3) accept differences in personal style and ability without criticizing or demeaning one another.

The job expectancy scale can be used to note the responsibilities of an entire team just as it can be used to define the initiative expected of individual subordinates.

More important still is settling on the decision-making procedures to be used within the team. Some groups work best when all decisions are made by consensus. That is a wonderful way to build commitment but it may slow the group because nothing can be done until everyone agrees. Other groups prefer majority decisions and rely on formal or informal votes. Still other groups prefer to rely on their leader for decisions, and some use all three procedures depending on the nature of the issue.

As you can imagine, there are advantages and disadvantages to all these procedures. The most important thing is making sure that everyone on the team understands what decisions will be made by each procedure. Taking time to discuss these issues at the start of the project will make it possible to avoid many difficulties later.

Making arrangements for periodic reports is the final step. Teams work best when they have regular meetings and you should help them establish a regular schedule. The nature of the project may determine how frequently the team meets. When deadlines are close at hand or conditions are changing rapidly, teams may meet on a daily—or even hourly—basis. Other projects suggest weekly or semiweekly meetings. There are few hard-and-fast rules, but groups meeting less than once a month may lose their identity. As a result, you should probably try to schedule meetings at least on a monthly basis, if only to keep the group intact.

Meetings are the object of many jokes and complaints in most professional circles. We all hear the "three too's": there are *too* many meetings, they last *too* long, and they accomplish *too* little. The sad thing is that these complaints are often justified.

Meetings that run on and on waste everyone's time and sap the team's energy. A simple well-prepared agenda is the best way to avoid the long, pointless gatherings that sometimes pass as meetings. To be most effective, the agenda should be distributed three to five days prior to the meeting so everyone can be prepared to deal with key issues. Agendas are so important that many senior managers refuse to attend meetings for which there is no agenda. I think the practice should become more popular.

Even a simple agenda is better than none. At the very least, the agenda should include the group name, scheduled date, time, and location, and a list of the topics to be discussed. The sample in Figure 2.5 is an acceptable form.

More sophisticated agendas like the one in Figure 2.6 add information that makes them even more valuable. Note that this agenda includes everything in the first while adding several important features. It shows who is expected to attend, who is responsible for each topic, what is to be accomplished in each area, and an estimated time for each item.

AGENDA
MARKETING SUPPORT GROUP
AUGUST 3, 1989
2:00 P.M.

Personnel Update
Facilities Support
Current Projects
Compensation Plan
Action Items

Figure 2.5. Sample agenda

AGENDA
MARKETING SUPPORT GROUP
AUGUST 3, 1989
2:00 P.M.

Team members: Mark Able, Karen Beach (chair), Sharon Coach, Steve Deal, Howard Fing, Alex Marks, Kevin Smith

Time	Item	Description
2:00—2:15	Personnel Update	Alex Marks will summarize recent changes in corporate personnel plans
2:15—2:25	Facilities Support	Steve Deal will report on proposed new facilities
2:25—2:50	Current Projects	Project leaders (Mark Able, Karen Beach, and Howard Fing) will report on current status of projects
2:50—3:15	Compensation Plan	Kevin Smith will present new compensation plan; team may accept as is, recommend changes, or reject proposal
3:15—3:30	Action Items	Karen Beach will assign action items for next week's meeting

Figure 2.6.   Sample agenda.

Managers looking at Figure 2.6 for the first time occasionally raise two objections. First, they say, "My people would never let me cut off discussion just because time was up. We ought to be able to talk long enough to make a good decision."

The objection is an important one, and I would never encourage you to cut off discussion before team members were satisfied. But discussions can run on for hours without making much progress. By suggesting a time limit, you encourage people to speak briefly and to the point. You can always relax the limit when the group needs more time, but more often than not team members will agree that enough has been said and will be anxious to get on to the next order of business.

The second objection is a little more complex. "What if someone wants to talk about something that's not on the agenda? Shouldn't we leave room for other business?" The answer is "yes" but you need to do it in a way that won't catch other members of the team off guard. If people don't feel they can talk about what's important to them, they probably won't work very hard for the group. On the other hand, too much "other business" will disrupt the flow of discussion and make it difficult to get anything else done. Worse yet, the things that show up under other business may interest only a few members, and others will be at a disadvantage because they haven't prepared for the discussion.

This situation can pose quite a dilemma, but sophisticated managers have developed a commonsense solution. Two or three days before distributing the agenda, they call all team members to see what topics should be included in the agenda. That tactic makes sure everyone feels part of the process. And developments in the few days prior to the meeting can be built in if the group as a whole feels that there is good reason to do so.

Conclusion

Delegation and coaching are vital parts of every manager's job. In this chapter, you have watched one manager develop the needed trust and you have seen how this fits into a general theory of the manager's role.

Delegation and coaching are closely related processes. Delegation requires selecting a capable person to do a job, explaining the task, giving the person needed authority, and making arrangements to keep in touch. Coaching is like teaching that takes place at each step of the process.

You have also been introduced to the job expectancy scale and seen how it can be used to make delegation and coaching less confusing. The chapter closed by showing that many of the same steps apply to working with project teams.

The case materials following this chapter show more practical applications of these concepts. The Sara Michaels story shows how a very successful manager used the job expectancy scale to start a process that overcame a number of problems. The dialog between John and Bill shows how even the simplest instructions can become confusing.

Suggested Readings

Blanchard, Kenneth, and Spencer Johnson. *The One Minute Manager.* New York: William Morrow and Company, 1982.

Blanchard, Kenneth, and Robert Lorber. *Putting the One Minute Manager to Work.* New York: Berkley Books, 1984.

Blanchard, Kenneth, Patricia Zigarmi, and Drea Zigarmi. *Leadership and the One Minute Manager.* New York: William Morrow and Company, 1985.

Bradford, David L., and Allan R. Cohen. *Managing for Excellence.* New York: John Wiley & Sons, 1984.

Doyle, Michael, and David Straus. *How to Make Meetings Work.* Chicago: The Playboy Press, 1976.

Fournies, Ferdinand F. *Coaching for Improved Work Performance.* Blue Ridge Summit, Pennsylvania: Liberty House, 1978.

Gilbreath, Robert D. *Winning at Project Management.* New York: John Wiley & Sons, 1986.

Janis, Irving L. *Group Think.* 2d ed., rev. Boston: Houghton Mifflin Company, 1983.

Jay, Antony. "How to Run a Meeting." *Harvard Business Review* (March–April 1976): 43–57.

Jewell, Linda N., and H. Joseph Reits. *Group Effectiveness in Organizations.* Glenview, Illinois: Scott, Foresman and Company, 1981.

Keys, Bernard, and Robert Bell. "Four Faces of the Fully Functioning Middle Manager." *California Management Review* 24 (Summer 1982): 59–67.

Lambert, Clark. *The Complete Book of Supervisory Training.* New York: John Wiley & Sons, 1984.

Levine, Harvey A. *Project Management Using Microcomputers.* Berkeley, California: Osborne McGraw-Hill, 1986.

McConkey, Dale D. *No-Nonsense Delegation.* rev. ed. New York: AMACOM, 1986.

Mayo, Edward J., and Lance P. Jarvis. "Delegation 101: Lessons from the White House." *Business Horizons* 31 (September–October 1988): 2–12.

Meredith, Jack R., and Samuel J. Mantel, Jr. *Project Management.* New York: John Wiley & Sons, 1985.

Ninomiya, J. S. "Wagon Masters and Lesser Managers." *Harvard Business Review* (March–April 1988): 84–90.

Odiorne, George S. *How Managers Make Things Happen.* 2d ed. Englewood Cliffs, New Jersey: Prentice-Hall, 1982.

Vroom, Victor V., and Philip W. Yetton. *Leadership and Decision Making.* Pittsburgh: University of Pittsburgh Press, 1973.

Case Studies:
Sara Michaels

Sara Michaels is a Regional Manager for a national office products wholesaler. Her region covers five states and her office is located in the central region warehouse. She shares the facility with the Regional Sales Manager, Regional Purchasing Manager, and Regional Delivery Manager.

Sara has been in this position for a little over a year and says that things are finally starting to come together. "I was put in this position," she explains, "as an emergency measure. Things were really falling apart. The previous Regional Manager was well respected but things just weren't working out. Competitors had carved out large chunks of our business and profits had fallen dramatically."

The rest of the story is told in Sara's own words.

During the first few weeks on the job, I spent most of my time trying to size up the problems. It became clear that our people weren't working together. Sales, Purchasing, and Delivery were like rival kingdoms, each fighting the other. The managers are good people but they just didn't seem to be able to work together. Sales was bringing in large orders for things we didn't stock; Purchasing was looking for "good buys" whether or not we had customers for the items; and Delivery was trying to get drivers on regular routes. As a result, customers were bailing out because we couldn't provide prompt delivery and frequently backlogged orders. Worse yet, our warehouse was filling up with items for which we didn't have a market.

Things were so bad when I first got here that I considered firing all three managers. Fortunately, our Personnel Representative got to me first. He pointed out that canning all three of them without giving them a chance to get it together would scare other people at a time when we couldn't afford to lose anybody.

Over the next few weeks, I spent long hours meeting with each of the three managers. Using the job expectancy scale, I found that each was doing about what he thought should be done. Bill Nichols in Purchasing even showed me several memoranda from the last Regional Manager directing him to purchase large stocks of underpriced items. For me, reading those memos was the key to understanding the problem. Each of the managers was looking at his operation without seeing how it affected other areas.

I formed a three-step plan to turn things around. I knew I had to get to the managers before the hard feelings between them got any worse. I had met with each of them individually so I decided it was time to pull them together. During our first meeting, I explained just how bad things were—the company was ready to close the warehouse, shift the inventory to an adjoining region, and lay off all our people. We could survive, I said, only if we all pulled together.

As a starting point, I wanted us to become the most efficient region in the company. They all agreed that that would be an impressive step. Finding ways to increase our efficiency forced the three of them to work together. Slowly but surely, I could see the results.

I knew I had turned the tables when Bill Nichols instructed his purchasing agents to survey sales representatives before making major buys. I took that as a sign that the top three managers were working together. It also meant that we would face a new problem: employees in each of the areas were so used to going on their own that they would have to learn a whole new way of doing their jobs.

Time for step two of my plan. At our next team meeting, I explained the techniques I had used to form our team: personal development conferences with each of the managers, followed by a team meeting. As we talked about the process, I could see that each of the managers was ready to begin working with their own people. Over the next few weeks each of the managers formed teams within their areas. And each team began formulating objectives that showed how they fitted into the region as a whole.

The area teams are working pretty well and results are starting to show on the bottom line. We've reduced overhead by 17 percent, sales are up 27 percent, and we expect profits to increase considerably as well.

I haven't moved on to step three yet because I want everyone to get used to the new order. At the same time, I don't want everyone to settle in. We've come a long way but I know we can do better. As soon as we can release the most recent profit figures I want to get cracking on the next step. I expect everyone to feel good about what we've accomplished and I plan to build on that basis by bringing together some cross-functional teams.

So far all of our teams have been defined by the members' jobs.

I have my senior managers' team, and each senior manager has a team in their areas. Cross-functional teams will bring together people from different areas. I don't know how many teams we will form, but I think I may try to get two or three more going by the end of the year. I want a mixed team from all three areas to begin looking at ways to improve customer service. And I want a mixed team from Delivery and Purchasing to start looking at warehouse operations. After they are up and running, I will start looking to form other teams as the need arises.

If I were to summarize our procedures in the simplest possible terms, I'd emphasize use of the job expectancy scale to get each person up to speed, followed by team-building to get the group as a whole working together. So far things have worked well for us and I plan to continue using the procedure.

Bill and John

Experience shows that even people who know each other well frequently misunderstand one another. The following dialog displays some of the problems that may arise. The first column shows what the speaker is saying while the second column shows how it is interpreted by the other person. You may want to cover the second column when you read it for the first time. During your second reading, see if you can find ways to avoid the misunderstandings.

Bill: Good morning, John. I'm glad to see you at your desk so early. I need to talk to you about the Myers project.

John: Well, here it comes—he's heard about problems with the Myers report and he's starting to keep track of my hours.

John: You know I'm always here by 7:30—and now with the Myers project taking up so much time, I'm often here earlier.

Bill: He's sure in a bad mood. Things must be worse than I thought.

Bill: Oh—do you think you'll be able to finish the final report by the end of the month?

John: Now he's giving me a deadline. It's not realistic but he's the boss.

John: I don't know—that will be awfully tight.

Bill: He's hedging again. I'd better get him to set a target date. We can always make changes as we get closer.

Bill: Well, let's give it an extra week. How about the seventh of next month?

John: That still doesn't give me enough time to get current figures; they won't be released for a week afterward. But if he wants it by the seventh, that's when he'll get it.

John: OK, I'll see what I can do.

Bill: I probably won't get much of a report by the seventh, but this will be a good chance for him to learn how to schedule projects.

Bill: Good. I'll look forward to getting the report.

Over the next several weeks, John worked long hours to finish the report. Although he was unable to get current statistics, he was able to make some good estimates. He was pleased with his work and proud to submit the report a day early.

John: Well, here's the Myers report. Do you want to look it over?

Bill: What's going on here? I didn't think he could possibly finish the report on time. I'd better look it over now so he knows I appreciate his effort.

Bill: [thumbing through the report] This is good, I mean really good!

John: Is that all he can say? I really busted my butt to get it done and he acts just like nothing special happened.

John: Thanks.

Bill: He doesn't sound very happy. I better give him a few more strokes.

Bill: [continuing to read] By the way, I see you've used estimates for the sales and revenue figures. That must have taken a lot of work. Why didn't you wait for the real numbers to come out next week?

John: What an SOB. He knew when the numbers would be released and he set the deadline so I couldn't possibly get them!

John: [becoming a bit defensive] *You* set the deadline; I did the best I could.

Bill: I don't like his attitude. He's acting like I'm responsible for his screw-up.

Bill: Whatever you say, but we will still have to revise this to reflect the actual figures.

John: This is bull! He set the deadline but now he is expecting me to cover his mistake. I bet he's going to blame me for the delay.

John: I don't think you know how much time I've put into this. My other work is backed up and I won't be able to spend any more time on this until the end of the month.

Bill: Now he's refusing to do his work. His attitude is worse than I thought. I'd better start looking for someone to replace him.

Bill: Well, if you say so, but the client won't be happy.

John: Just as I thought; he's going to blame me. I better get my resumé out and see what else is available.

3

Overcoming Performance Problems
A Primer on Leadership and Motivation

Surveys indicate that, on average, workers in this country believe they need to work at only 40 percent of capacity. This is a sad commentary because most employees start out as eager workers. As they put in time, they learn that hard work and real commitment seldom pay. They say managers ignore their accomplishments, badger them when they make an error, and reward them—if at all— for not rocking the boat.

In turn, managers complain that workers are unmotivated, blame unions—or the government—for protecting incompetent employees, and struggle to make do by assigning important projects to the few "good ones."

Both the angry cynicism of employees and the bitter resignation of managers have their roots in poor communication. Time and again, studies show that neither fully understand how their jobs are seen by the others. Managers ignore subordinates' accomplishments that are not "part of the job," while subordinates toil to "just keep the plant running." Sadly, managers and subordinates seem to understand one another best in the first six months after the subordinate is hired. Thereafter, their relationships decay until reaching an uneasy truce, or until one of them can no longer live with the situation. Only extraordinary interventions ease the tension, and decay begins again once the intervention ends.

This chapter introduces a model of motivation that makes it possible to anticipate and diagnose performance problems. The chapter then looks at three common performance problems and introduces techniques designed to overcome them.

Listen to any group of successful managers describe make-or-break moments in their careers. You are likely to hear many similar stories. Time after time, the stories center on subordinates who just weren't getting the job done. The following tales are typical of many you might hear.

I really didn't know what to do. I had just transferred into the division and this was my first managerial job. Dealing with "old Joe" was the hardest part.

The guy was twenty years my senior and it seemed like he had been in the company forever. He was kind of an institution, if you know what I mean.

Everybody liked him and we got along fine—as long as I didn't ask him to do anything. I'm still not sure how he spent his time because I didn't see him finish a single project while I was there. Work piled up on his desk until someone else took over or until it was too late to do anything with it. Week after week, meeting after meeting, he reported "good progress" but nothing ever got done.

Things were going pretty well when I first took over as Regional Manager. Our products were about the best available, and we were busy just taking orders from our regular customers.

Then a new company started doing business in the region. Their products weren't any better than ours and their prices were about 10 percent higher. I didn't expect much trouble because I figured our regular customer base would more than make up for all their advertising.

I couldn't figure it out when we started losing customers. Even some of our regulars switched. I started calling around and found that the new guys were beating us on service—same day delivery on in-stock orders, no-questions-asked on returns, and big discounts on delayed orders.

I knew we could do just as well as they did, but nobody on my team really seemed to care. I mean, I really put it on the line. I talked until I was blue in the face. I explained what the new company was doing, and I showed how we could match their service. All we needed to do was work a little bit harder. No big deal, just 10 percent more effort. But nobody, *not one person*, was willing to support me. I might as well have been alone in the region for all of the help I got.

I learned more about motivation in six months working with the R&D types than in six years of college. These guys were really off the wall. They'd sit around and do nothing for weeks at a time. Then they seemed to catch fire; they would work night and day for ten, twelve, fourteen days—however long it took to finish their projects.

It didn't seem to matter what they were working on, even if it was something with no commercial value, even if no one else in the company was interested. These guys would ignore everything else—they even ignored directions from the GM—while they tinkered with their gadgets. You could dock their pay, cancel vacations, threaten to can them—they just didn't seem to care about anything but their pet projects.

It took me six months to figure out how to work with them. That was probably the toughest time in my life but I couldn't have asked for a better learning experience.

Problems like these are part of every manager's life. Learning how to solve them is an important career step. Successful managers learn how to cope with them without resorting to threats, verbal abuse, or terminations. Much of what we call leadership is the ability to overcome performance problems and get a group of people working together for their common benefit. Doing this calls for a clear understanding of the dynamics of performance problems.

Leadership can be felt throughout an organization. It gives pace and energy to the work and empowers the workforce. Empowerment is the collective effect of leadership. . . . Where there are leaders, work is stimulating, challenging, fascinating, and fun.
—Warren Bennis, *Why Leaders Can't Lead* (San Francisco: Jossey-Bass Publishers, 1989), pp. 22–23.

The Anatomy of Performance Problems

"Performance problem" is a general name that we use to label a variety of situations. Each of the stories above refers to a performance problem but you might have to look closely to see what these situations have in common.

Seeing the common thread in these situations is important because it opens the way to understanding some fundamental points about motivation and leadership.

In the most general terms, a performance problem exists when one or more employees is not working up to a manager's expectations. In the examples above, "Old Joe" kept working at a pace that satisfied earlier managers. At least they found it easier to accept him than to do something about his work habits. He had become an institution by satisfying them, but failed to adapt to the new manager who expected more. The "lazy" regional crew was unwilling to work "even a little harder" to meet the challenge presented by the new competitor. And the R&D group seemed to work only on projects of interest to them, despite threats and other pressure from management.

In each of these descriptions, we see only one side of the story. The employees might describe the situations in very different terms. Old Joe might say that the new manager had unreasonable expectations and didn't give him enough credit for what he was doing. The regional staff might say it was unreasonable to expect them to match the new competitor without added support. And the R&D crew may well laugh at managers who expect them to work on trivial projects when there is interesting work to do.

Fortunately, we don't have to side with either the managers or the employees. We can simply say that a performance problem exists when the employees' performance doesn't come up to the manager's expectations.

Of course there are some cases of simple misunderstanding. The employees are actually working up to the manager's expectations but their performance is never recognized. This situation can result from poor measurement systems or from managerial inattention. But such cases are relatively easy to correct and shouldn't distract us from the central issue: motivation. When employees are not performing in a manner consistent with the manager's expectations, it's time to look closely at the problem of motivation.

A General Theory of Motivation

Motivation is one of the hot topics in management seminars. That comes as no surprise because it has been on top of the list for some time. Motivation is also one of the most researched topics in management literature. Library shelves are full of books about motivation and journal articles summarizing the latest findings. Fortunately, the central concepts are relatively simple and consistent with most people's experiences. Let's look at another example.

Karen supervises a group of data entry clerks. The clerks are expected to enter information at the rate of 12,000 keystrokes per hour. That figure is the minimum acceptable level of activity according to the experts who designed the system, and research indicates that it is a reasonable expectation. In fact, some clerks are able to enter information at twice that rate and a few can work even faster.

Karen was concerned about the amount of work her group was producing and began monitoring their output. She wasn't surprised by the findings. Even though they were well trained and familiar with the equipment, the clerks in her group were averaging between 3,000 and 5,000 keystrokes per hour—less than half of the accepted *minimum* standard.

After several attempts to motivate her employees, Karen called in an outside consultant. "They just aren't motivated," was the way she explained the problem. The consultant spent several afternoons watching the clerks and it certainly seemed that Karen was right. Each clerk moved in slow motion. In the morning, it took them over a half hour to get things out of their desks and set up their work areas. Getting files from central cabinets seemed to take an eternity as the clerks shuffled to and from their desks, stopping to talk to everyone they met. Phone conversations were stretched to the limit, and coffee breaks seemed to last for hours.

Most people watching the group would agree with Karen's conclusion—these workers simply weren't motivated. Fortunately, the consultant had seen groups like this before and had a hunch about what was happening. Forty-five minutes before the end of their shifts, the clerks turned off their machines and began slowly clearing their work areas. Files were returned to the central cabinets one at a time. Every step seemed to take an eternity, and the clerks moved like creatures in a low-budget horror film.

Curiously, something magical happened at quitting time. The dead came to life and the clerks that barely had energy to breathe during the day were transformed into active, dynamic beings. One raced to meet her boyfriend. Another rushed off to a computer class and a third hurried out to a PTA meeting. In fact, once the workday was finished, all of the clerks turned into vigorous, enthusiastic people.

Although extreme, this example makes an important point about motivation. To Karen, the employees appeared unmotivated because they weren't doing what she wanted. But viewed from beyond Karen's position, it is clear that the employees are motivated. They are motivated by things outside the work situation. One is motivated by the chance to spend time with her boyfriend, another by her computer class, and a third by her involvement with the PTA. Generalizing from this example, we can say that everyone is motivated by something. Unfortunately, our language gets us in trouble in some other cases. Because motivate is an active verb, it sounds like something managers have to do *to* people. In fact, motivation is something that all people have. Managers just have to find out what it is. Once managers understand what motivates their people, tapping in is pretty easy.

The most important thing I ever learned about being a manager is also the most straightforward. I keep it on a notecard inside my desk drawer so that I never forget it: NO ONE EVER WORKS FOR YOU. THEY ALWAYS WORK FOR THEMSELVES. SUCCESSFUL MANAGERS MAKE PEOPLE WANT TO DO WHAT THE MANAGER NEEDS THEM TO DO.
—An experienced manager

Employees' Motives

Finding out what motivates employees is an ongoing task. Fortunately there is a great deal of research to guide us. (For a useful summary of this research, see Kenneth A. Kovack, "What Motivates Employees? Workers and Supervisors Give Different Answers," *Business Horizons* (September–October 1987), pp. 58–65.)

Beginning in 1946, a series of studies has sought to identify the concerns that motivate employees. Anyone reading these studies is likely to notice two things. First, employees consistently emphasize what many people call "higher motives." Interesting work, appreciation for work done, and a feeling of "being in" on things top most employees' lists.

The second thing most readers notice is how frequently managers misunderstand their employees' motives. Managers usually say that employees are motivated by wages, security, and good working conditions. While these items are rated highly by younger workers and those with limited incomes, they do not accurately characterize the primary motives of most employees.

Even dividing workers into general categories by age, income, sex, and organizational level doesn't tell the whole story. Each employee is an individual with his or her own interests and concerns. To manage people effectively, you need to know what matters to each.

Knowing what motivates each employee is an essential part of the process. At the same time, this also forces you to confront one of the fundamental paradoxes of management. As a manager, you are responsible for the performance of your people, but you never really control them. Each chooses to work or not, to push themselves or relax, to cooperate or resist direction. And each makes these choices in terms of something over which you have no control: their personal motives.

What then can you control? How can you motivate a group to improve their performance? The answer to these questions rests in factors over which you do have some control: your group's mission and the opportunities you create.

Organizational Mission

Mission is a term used to describe a group or organization's purpose or reason for being. Charles Garfield describes a mission as "the call to action, the 'click' that starts things moving." (Charles Garfield, *Peak Performers* [New York: William Morrow and Company, 1986], p. 31.)

We could give more precise definitions, but they wouldn't change the basic point. A mission is a sense of purpose or a reason for striving. We can see them at all levels in truly outstanding organizations.

At the highest levels, missions describe the direction of whole companies. "Building for a better tomorrow," "quality is job one," "restoring America's competitiveness," "computers so sophisticated they're easy to use," and "technology at the service of humanity" are catch phrases that translate their parent companies' missions into simple, memorable terms.

Just as missions provide direction for whole companies, missions also drive each unit within the organization. "Same day service," "zero defects," and "service with a smile" characterize the missions of units within larger organizations.

It is even possible to talk about missions at the lowest levels of organizations. A cafeteria crew might promise "never a dirty table," or a technician might aim to "keep the computer in operation twenty-four hours a day." These missions may not seem as impressive as the corporate missions, but they serve the same function. They have value to the participants and they give meaning to the work.

Missions that give meaning to work share three characteristics. First, they call for growth, change, or development. The sense of movement is exciting and gives participants something to shoot for.

Second, missions have a sense of value to the participants. Missions differ from corporate strategies by focusing attention on factors beyond financial measures. While investors might be satisfied by purely financial measures of performance, few employees are. Missions reflect this fact by looking to social values that make participants feel good about their jobs and about themselves.

Finally, missions often aim for superlative performance. They use phrases like "superior," "outstanding," and "the best." In this way, missions present a challenge, something beyond business-as-usual. Properly stated missions encourage high levels of performance by creating a standard of excellence to which employees can aspire.

Opportunities to Achieve

Opportunity is the final piece of the motivation puzzle. "Opportunity" is a convenient shorthand expression that refers to what people believe will happen if they work hard.

Opportunity is a positive factor when people believe hard work will help them satisfy their motives. Opportunity is also positive when people believe hard work will help them accomplish an important mission. And you can expect the highest level of performance when people believe hard work will satisfy their motives *and* accomplish an important mission.

That sounds like an ideal situation. In many respects it is. For example, think about Judy, a pharmaceutical saleswoman. She works on commission, so high sales volume contributes to her personal goal: saving money for her son's college education. If one of her products is an important new drug that promises to reduce deaths from cancer, high sales volume also contributes to an important mission: saving lives. In addition, the drug is reasonably priced, there are abundant supplies, her company has a good reputation, and her territory includes many physicians willing to prescribe the drug. Put together, these factors create opportunities for Judy to sell large quantities of the drug.

A diagram depicting Judy's situation might look like the one in Figure 3.1. In this diagram, motives, mission, and opportunities overlap because the three fit together well. Some people talk about the three being aligned. This technical term is used whenever behaviors that contribute to one of the three components also contribute to the others.

Even in this nearly ideal situation, the overlap isn't complete. There are still several areas where Judy's motives, the organization's mission, and the opportunities are not perfectly aligned. For example, Judy wants to spend more time with her family. This creates pressure for her to reduce the number of sales calls she makes and works against the corporate mission.

Other factors can also reduce alignment. For example, the company might decide to increase short-term returns by raising prices

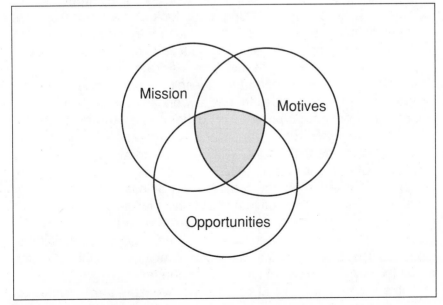

Figure 3.1. Motives in alignment

and limiting supplies. This would reduce opportunities for sales, conflicting with Judy's motives and the stated mission.

The important point to remember is that you can expect high levels of performance where the motives of the individual, mission of the organization, and opportunites support the same behaviors. Problems arise when there is little overlap among these three factors. Let's look at some typical problem situations.

Performance Problem One:
The Lazy Subordinate

Almost every manager's problem list includes a lazy, unreliable subordinate. John is typical. He is talented and capable, but just doesn't seem to care about the job. Although there is no evidence of substance abuse or unmanageable personal problems, he simply isn't making much effort at work. John arrives late, leaves early, takes long lunches, and does as little as possible while on the job.

John's performance is a drag on the group, and other people in the group are beginning to think they can get away with the same behaviors.

Most managers respond to this situation by asking what's wrong with John. The answer is nothing. Let's look at the three elements of the motivation process to see what clues they offer.

First, we don't know a great deal about John's motives but we can make some educated guesses. The desire for accomplishment doesn't seem to drive him, and he doesn't appear to be working for promotion. He may value his friends at work and probably needs his salary, but he might surprise us on either count. And he seems to value his time away from work—since it is growing day by day.

Mission is the second factor. Without even knowing what it is, we can see that it doesn't mean much to John. He might say the right things when asked about the company and its mission, but it is clear that the mission has not motivated him to high levels of performance.

Finally, we need to look at opportunities. They may be a negative factor, since the situation permits John to do what he wants without regard to the mission of the company. A diagram of this situation would look like the one in Figure 3.2 on the facing page.

In this case, motives and opportunity overlap—the individual is doing what he wants—but there is no overlap between motives and

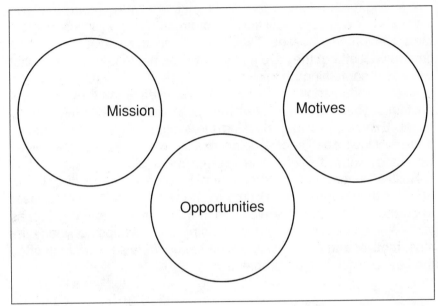

Figure 3.2. Motives out of alignment

mission. John is not contributing to the group's mission, and the mission is not encouraging him to perform at acceptable levels. This is not a problem for John, but it clearly is for the manager. We will look at some possible solutions in a minute or two.

Performance Problem Two: The Hostile Subordinate

Hostile, angry subordinates represent a different sort of problem. While lazy subordinates never seem to get things done, hostile subordinates are often very productive. Unfortunately, their work is accompanied by a great deal of complaining. Here is how one manager described a hostile subordinate.

> Her work is really great, once she gets around to it. The hard part is putting up with all the griping and whining. Nothing is ever done well enough to satisfy her: we don't have enough clerical help, her office needs cleaning, no one is taking care of her research funds. You name one of our systems and she has found something wrong with it. Sometimes, she gets so bad that I feel like hiding so I don't have to face her.

A strong, unpredictable temper is another sign of anger. In meetings and elsewhere, hostile subordinates snipe at convenient targets, even their bosses. They usually apologize once they've had time to cool off but they are just as likely as not to take another shot whenever something annoys them.

Hostility often shows up in other ways, even when they don't say anything. Their behavior often seems to be self-defeating or irrational. Examples include bucking the system, inattention to detail, and malicious obedience—doing exactly what they are told, even when they know it will have embarrassing results.

Hostile subordinates are sometimes tough to figure out. To an outsider they appear to be doing all the wrong things. They appear to be their own worst enemies and in many cases they are. But, as you will see in a moment, understanding relationships between mission, motive, and opportunity *as the subordinate sees them* is often the key to resolving the problem.

Performance Problem Three: Ineffective Teams

Both of the performance problems we've looked at so far involve individuals. And, as you will see in a minute, both can be solved by working with the individuals. A different sort of problem may arise when a group or team is involved.

During the 1960s and 1970s, American managers heard a great deal about superior Japanese methods. These methods frequently used groups or teams to solve problems and make decisions. The teams were composed of workers from all levels and all specialties who were brought together to investigate problems and find solutions.

Many American managers were so impressed by the benefits of team management that they rushed to take advantage of them. In some cases, hastily assembled teams were able to accomplish a great deal. In other cases, using teams was a draw of sorts. The teams didn't accomplish very much, but they didn't cost very much either. Finally, in some cases, team approaches were unmitigated disasters. Valuable resources (time and money) were wasted, their "solutions" actually created worse problems, and some team meetings created so many hard feelings that participants could never again work together.

Of course, most team results fall somewhere between the extremes. However, it is clear that teams can create unique performance problems. One characteristic of these problems is particularly frustrating for managers.

By themselves, each member of the team can be skilled, knowledgeable, and cooperative. However, nothing seems to go right when the members get together. One frustrated manager's description is as good as any you will find in the textbooks.

> It was the strangest thing I have ever seen. I picked the brightest and most cooperative members of my group. They were all experienced and they all knew the importance of the project.
>
> But the team simply never worked—things went wrong at our first meeting and they never got any better. One member sat in the corner—I mean really sat in the corner—and took verbal shots at everyone else. Two members locked horns over every decision and nobody could get anything done until they were satisfied. Golf scores seemed to be the only thing of interest to the other members.
>
> I don't know how anyone else feels, but I can tell you I will never again assemble a project team if I can avoid it!

That is not a pretty picture, but it is probably repeated more than many managers care to admit.

The important thing to note is that the problems didn't show up until the individuals became a team. By themselves, the individuals were ideal employees. As a group, the results were disastrous. This is typical of team problems; they are problems with the way the group works, not problems of the individual members.

Personal Development Conferences

We have looked at three typical performance problems: lazy subordinates, hostile subordinates, and ineffective teams. The first two are individual problems and may be addressed through personal development conferences. The third is a group problem and requires team building, an approach we will discuss in the next section.

Personal development conferences are one-on-one meetings that you can call whenever you encounter an individual performance problem. Identifying the cause of performance problems and developing solutions are the primary purposes for personal development conferences.

Personal development conferences can be fairly time-consuming—especially if you have several subordinates with performance problems. Even one subordinate with several persistent performance problems can take a great deal of time. As a result, some managers prefer to use performance appraisals to work out solutions.

Although I have known many successful managers who use performance appraisals instead of personal development conferences, I discourage this practice. So much is at stake in an appraisal interview that the subordinate may never feel comfortable discussing the problem frankly and openly. Moreover, the fact that appraisals are often tied to salary considerations means that many subordinates become defensive whenever problems are mentioned. As a result, you can get far more done if you call a conference specifically to discuss the performance problem.

Pick a time that is convenient for both you and the subordinate. Whenever possible, choose a time when neither of you will be rushed, and by all means pick a location where you won't be overheard. Begin by explaining why you have asked the subordinate to meet with you. An introduction like the following will work well most of the time:

Good morning, John.
    Thanks for joining me for coffee. Let me tell you what I want to discuss. We've worked together for nearly two years and things have gone pretty smoothly for most of that time. In the last week or two I've noticed something that I think might be a problem and I wanted to talk it through with you before it gets out of hand.

Many subordinates will begin volunteering information at this point but others may feel threatened. In either case, you should be prepared to characterize the problem, as you see it, and give the subordinate a chance to describe things from his or her point of view. Remember, the object of the conference is finding a solution. You can do that most effectively if you understand the problem *as the subordinate sees it*. This means that you will have to do a lot of listening. You may even hear some things about yourself that you don't like. However, if the conference is going to accomplish anything, you need to listen carefully and attentively.

Your nonverbal behavior will tell subordinates whether or not you are really interested in their concerns. If your behavior shows you don't really want to hear their views, most subordinates will simply assume that you are practicing something you read in the latest "how to be a great manager" book. They will clam up or disguise their real feelings. On the other hand, if your nonverbal behavior conveys real interest and respect for them as persons, you have a pretty good chance of finding out what is really bothering them.

Occasionally, a subordinate will deny that there is a problem. "I've just had a lot on my mind lately" and "It's just a small personal problem" are two common responses. Both are probably actual causes of performance problems. However, you still need to find a solution and you should be prepared to summarize the problem as you see it. You might proceed as follows:

> I know that personal problems can affect things at work, John, but I have a feeling that there may be more involved. Let me tell you what I mean. I have had a hard time working with you for the last two weeks because you seem so eager to disagree with me. For example, yesterday you got really worked up about the delay in printing business cards. I know it's an annoyance, but it doesn't seem like something to be that angry about.

This is a good time to pause and let the subordinate speak. And remember, there is no reason to hurry. Some subordinates will be reluctant to speak and some will have difficulty putting their feelings into words. Once they start talking, you may even have to help them by using some probes like those you use in conducting selection interviews.

As the subordinate speaks, you should be able to form a pretty clear picture of the problem from his or her point of view. Here are some responses you might hear.

> Working here is just so frustrating. Every time I get a major project going, something goes wrong and we lose support. I can't think of a single time I have gotten the support I've been promised.

> This used to be a really great place to work—we had time to get to know each other and management really seemed to care about our feelings. Now it's just work, work, work. Everybody acts like we're just machines.

Frankly, you have had me on some pretty boring projects. I mean, who really cares if we are able to reduce variances by one ten-thousandth of an inch. The old specs worked just fine and I don't see any reason to push for so much precision.

Some managers would be angry to hear these responses, but you should be glad the subordinate has been open with you. Think about these responses in terms of motives, mission, and opportunities.

How do you suppose the first person sees the working environment? To me it sounds like he is saying that he isn't being given an opportunity to do his job correctly. The second person has revealed some motives that may be inconsistent with the job. He seems to want social contact and a caring, nurturing environment. The third person appears to doubt the mission to which she has been assigned.

If these readings are correct, you can begin to see how to deal with each. The first person needs to be convinced that there really is an opportunity to get his job done. You could do that by providing additional support, or by showing him how to get things done without additional support.

There are several approaches you might use in dealing with the second person. Traditional, hard-line managers might try to convince him that his expectations are unreasonable. I can almost hear a real hard case I once met saying "you're here to work, meet your friends on your own time." Of course, you are within your rights to respond that way, but it may not get the results you want. Other possibilities include involving the subordinate in projects with a great deal of opportunity for socializing or helping him find other social outlets.

You may also remind him of other motives associated with the job. For example, you might point out the following:

You are right, John. Things have changed but we didn't have any choice. If we hadn't tightened things up, the company would be out of business. As it is now, we have some really interesting projects and our wages are among the best around.

Of course that strategy will be persuasive only if the subordinate values interesting work and high salary. But you get the point.

The final person doesn't see the importance of "one ten-thousandth of an inch." And, you have to admit, she may be right.

If the extra precision is unrelated to an important mission, it is unrealistic to expect her to invest much effort. On the other hand, if the precision is vital to the mission, your best strategy is to explain its importance. You might say something like this.

> I know just how you feel. I felt the same way when I saw the new specs for the first time. Let me tell you what I found out when I talked to the engineers.

If your explanation is credible, you may have solved the problem. You can always fall back on more traditional answers ("do it that way because I say so") if your explanation doesn't work. But it wouldn't be so easy to explain things if you began by relying on authority.

These examples display some important techniques for dealing with performance problems. Once you know what the situation is as the subordinate sees it, you can use any of several strategies. You can

1. change the situation to create more opportunities
2. show the subordinate that there are opportunities that are being overlooked
3. try to convince the subordinate that his or her expectations are unrealistic
4. change the job to give the person more interesting tasks
5. suggest other ways of satisfying unfulfilled motives
6. draw on other motives
7. change your expectations
8. change the mission
9. explain the mission
10. explain expected tasks in terms of the mission

Not all of these techniques will work in every situation, but I would be surprised if there were very many cases where one or more of them won't work. The key is understanding the situation as the subordinate sees it, and identifying the subordinate's motives. Use personal development conferences to get information and develop solutions.

Team Building: Leading a Work Group

Working with a team raises problems similar to those encountered in working with individuals. However, there are some problems that are really group problems, problems that surface only when members of the group try to work together.

There is another complication as well. People are less likely to talk freely in a group, especially if they feel threatened or are unsure how their remarks will be interpreted. This means that you will have to work doubly hard to establish an appropriate climate. However, once you have gotten over that hurdle, you can think of a team-building session as a personal development conference for a whole group.

Many books and articles have been written about team building. We don't have time to summarize them here, but our understanding of motivation makes it easy to pick out the key points.

Call the group together and explain that you want to depart from the normal agenda. You see a problem in the way the team is working and you want everyone's help in resolving it. You need to be very careful here to avoid blaming any one individual. Focus attention on the way the group *as a whole* is working and explain that you want to develop procedures to avoid difficulties in the future. You might explain things like this:

> Good morning.
> Before we get started, I'd like to take some time to make sure we're on track. At our last meeting, I noticed a couple of things that made me a little uneasy. It didn't seem like everyone was really interested in our work and I had a feeling that we hadn't really focused our efforts.
> I'd like to make sure we hear from everyone. So, for a minute or two, I'd like each of you to think about your concerns. Then I'll go around the group and make a list. I want to make sure we have a complete list before discussing any part of it, so I'll ask you to save discussion until we finish this step. To make sure we get everything down, I'm going to put the list on the flip chart.

After team members have had a minute or two to think, turn to the first person and start making a list of their concerns. Your writing should be large enough for everyone to read and you may need to use several flip chart pages. A blackboard can also be used. Some members may be anxious to argue with others' interpretations so you will need to be polite but firm. Discourage discussion until you have heard from everyone.

Most problems in teams are predictable. Here are some of the more common responses.

I don't really feel like wasting my time. We've tried this before and the company never approved any of our ideas.

I've tried hard to find some solutions, but nobody ever listens to me. I'd have a solution tomorrow if you would only turn things over to me.

The real problem is Jan. She's talking all the time even though she doesn't have anything to say.

We sure waste a lot of time. Nobody really cares about this and I can't imagine why we're (or "I'm") here.

These are pretty direct comments and you may have to control some tempers. However, you will hear variations on these comments whenever there is a real problem with a team. The comments may be couched in more polite language, but you need to hear them to solve the problems.

Looking at these comments in terms of mission, motives, and opportunities gives you a key to solving the performance problems. Let's look at each of them in turn.

The first comment often comes from someone who is inactive or easily distracted. It is a partially hidden way of saying, "This is an important project" (good mission) and "I would really like to contribute" (positive motive) but "The company won't let us do anything about it" (no opportunity).

Working with an individual, you would try to explain that there really is an opportunity, or you might change the situation to create an opportunity. With a group you have an added advantage. You can enlist group support to convince the individual or you can ask the group for help creating opportunities. You might ask, "What can we do to make sure our suggestions are not ignored?"

The second comment often comes from persons protecting their status or ego. It is a transparent way of saying "I could do this all by myself and I don't understand why you won't let me." It is easy to see their primary motive—making sure everyone else knows how bright, talented, or capable they are. You can also see this motive in people who are constantly bickering, disagreeing, or taking shots at other members of the team.

This problem is a bit tougher to deal with in a group situation, especially when other members become hostile or angry. The trick is to explain things in a way that reassures such persons they are members of the team *because* they are bright, talented, and capable. That way they understand that working with the group is the best way of fulfilling their motive.

A personal attack like the one in comment three usually evidences a power struggle. Whoever made the comment sees Jan as a threat and wants to neutralize her. Other members of the group may become hostile and you can bet someone will leap to Jan's defense.

Here again, it is clear that the individual's motive is self-promotion. The person is really saying, "I deserve to be the leader/do most of the talking/be the center of attention." And here again, the best way to deal with the problem is to reassure the individual. Help the person see that being a productive member is the best way to get recognition.

Finally, comment four could reveal either of two concerns. Either the mission isn't valuable to the individual or the project doesn't satisfy any important motives. Sometimes both factors are involved.

You can deal with this situation using the same strategies you used with an individual. And you have the added advantage of group support. Tackle the mission first. Do other team members believe the mission is important? If yes, they can help you convince the dissident. If no, you should change or clarify the mission, especially since you need group support.

Dealing with the individual's motives in a group situation can be tricky. The best approach is to explain why you thought the person would benefit from membership on the team (growth, personal development, interesting work). Other members of the group can also suggest ways the individual will benefit, and their support can save the day.

If you can't find a way to associate the individual's motives with the project, you have learned an important lesson—you have learned what happens when you aren't careful in picking team members. When that happens, it's time to backtrack: replace the individual if possible or call in a personal favor by asking the person to stay with the group as a favor to you.

Conclusion

This chapter has looked at the role of leadership in overcoming performance problems. You have seen that a performance problem exists whenever a person's behavior doesn't match another person's expectations. Motivation is an appropriate concern if the expectations are proper and the behavior correctly understood.

Three factors are involved in motivation: the individual's motives, the group or organizational mission, and opportunities to achieve. Motives are said to be aligned when behaviors that contribute to the individual's motives are consistent with the group or organizational mission and the opportunities provided. Performance problems generally arise when these factors are not aligned, and efforts to correct the problem may focus on any one or all of the factors.

Common performance problems include lazy subordinates, hostile subordinates, and ineffective teams. Managers may deal with these problems by using personal development conferences and/or team-building strategies.

The Carol Arnold case following this chapter illustrates these principles by focusing on a complex situation in which individual motives may be at odds with the group mission. Finding a way to get everyone back on track is the central problem to solve.

Suggested Readings

Belbin, R. Meredith. *Management Teams*. New York: John Wiley & Sons, 1981.

Bennis, Warren, and Burt Nanus. *Leaders*. New York: Harper & Row, 1985.

Burns, James MacGregor. *Leadership*. New York: Harper & Row, 1978.

Garfield, Charles. *Peak Performers*. New York: William Morrow and Company, 1986.

Jewell, Linda N., and H. Joseph Reitz. *Group Effectiveness in Organizations*. Glenview, Illinois: Scott, Foresman and Company, 1981.

Kanter, Rosabeth Moss. *Change Masters*. New York: Simon and Schuster, 1983.

Maccoby, Michael. *Why Work: Leading the New Generation*. New York: Simon and Schuster, 1988.

Mertzger, Robert O. *Profitable Consulting: Guiding America's Managers into the Next Century*. Reading, Massachusetts: Addison-Wesley Publishing Company, 1989.

Rosenbaum, Bernard L. *How to Motivate Today's Workers*. New York: McGraw-Hill Book Company, 1982.

Tarkenton, Fran, and Tad Tuleja. *How to Motivate People*. New York: Harper & Row, 1986.

Woodcock, Mike, and Dave Francis. *Organisation* [sic] *Development Through Teambuilding*. New York: John Wiley & Sons, 1981.

Ziglar, Zig. *Top Performance*. New York: Berkley Books, 1986.

Case Study:
Carol Arnold

Carol Arnold supervises the grounds crew at a small, private business college. She has been in this job for several years and has generally good relationships with the five grounds keepers who report to her.

Until recently, life has been good to members of the grounds crew. The school is small, the students are friendly and cooperative, and there are few visitors on campus. "This is more like a family gathering than a job," is the way one of the grounds keepers described his job. In fact, the opportunity to socialize with students and faculty was one of the most attractive parts of the job. On sunny days, students and faculty members frequently met outside and it was not unusual to see grounds keepers joining in on discussions.

Things began to change dramatically a few months ago. The school had difficulty meeting its payroll commitments one month, and the Board of Trustees began reviewing finances in detail. They were not pleased by the results of their review.

For several years, the school's Finance Manager had adroitly shifted funds from one account to another. The shifting had made it possible to cover expenses, but it had also disguised the fact that several programs had been losing money. Things had finally gotten so bad that he could no longer cover the shortfall.

Acting to stave off a crisis, the Board directed the President to place the Finance Manager on leave and hire an interim replacement. The new Financial Manager took several weeks to study the school's situation and reported back to the President that only an immediate 25 percent cut in expenses would prevent bankruptcy. In addition, he said, long-term revenue projections were not positive, and the school needed to begin an aggressive marketing campaign.

Acting on the Finance Manager's recommendations, the President instructed all area directors to cut expenses by 30 percent immediately. He also hired a marketing firm to begin promoting the school by bringing potential students to campus. Within the next month, pedestrian traffic on campus increased by 30 percent as large numbers of potential students began attending several receptions.

Carol faced a series of tough decisions as a result of the President's action. Since almost all of her expenses were for salary, terminating two employees was the only way she could reduce costs. In addition, the increasing foot traffic on campus increased the amount of work for grounds keepers. Worse yet, the presence of so many potential students made it essential to present a good image.

Realizing that she had no alternatives, Carol terminated the two grounds keepers with the least seniority. Both were popular and both were good workers. Now she faced the problem of getting the remaining three grounds keepers to do more than ever before.

Reviewing their personnel folders, Carol began thinking about the task ahead.

John Howard was the senior grounds keeper. At 48, he had been with the school since he graduated from high school—almost 30 years. John was a quiet family man with two grown children and a third about to graduate from college. He owned his own home and three rental houses that provided a healthy income in addition to his salary. He was one of the most loyal employees and frequently attended receptions and other gatherings for faculty and staff members.

Steve Carlson was next in line of seniority. He had spent several years in the Army before joining the school. He was 37 and had been with the school for almost 12 years. Carol knew almost nothing about his personal life. A confirmed bachelor, Steve took a great deal of pride in his two cars—one an expensive imported sports car and the other an aging but large luxury sedan. No one knew how he bought the cars, but many people suspected he worked at least one and perhaps two other jobs.

Mark Downing was the remaining grounds keeper. Recently married with one child on the way, Mark had been with the school for 4 years. Twenty-three years of age, Mark was an active sportsman and took his vacation time in small pieces to go hunting and fishing on long weekends. He seldom socialized with other staff members, and Carol had never seen him at a school function. He even skipped the annual Christmas parties to spend time with his parents in an adjoining state.

In the past, Carol had talked to each of the grounds keepers about their careers. John had laughed when she used the word *career*. "You mean 'job,' don't you?" he asked. "I'm just doing this to keep busy until my kids graduate and my wife retires. Then we're going to travel."

Steve had been reluctant to talk. "You're the boss," he said. "You tell me what to do and I'll get it done. I don't really want to spend a lot of time talking about something that doesn't make any difference anyway." Carol had to admit that his work was as good as any but she was concerned about the attitude he expressed.

Finally, Mark was a little less sure of himself. "I don't know where I will wind up," he said. "I like what I do—I mean I really enjoy the people I work with, but I don't think I'm going to stay a grounds keeper forever. John seems happy but I could never spend 30 years at the same place."

Carol now has to explain the terminations and make new work assignments. How should she proceed?

4

Appraising Subordinate Performance

Performance appraisal is the heart of personnel systems in almost all organizations. The overwhelming majority of large and small corporations use appraisal systems. Federal and state government agencies also use appraisal systems and most cities do too. The majority use appraisals to set compensation levels, counsel employees, and identify training needs. Other uses include selecting employees for promotion, planning to meet manpower needs, retention and discharge, and validation of selection procedures.

Although most organizations have appraisal systems, few have produced promised results. Well-meaning but unskilled managers compromise many systems. Recurrent errors include leniency, central tendency, and halo. It seems that favored employees can do no wrong while others are seldom rewarded for their efforts. Managers in turn are often penalized when they take appraisal systems seriously and criticize the work of long-term employees. Is it any wonder that managers and employees alike react with anger, distrust, and cynicism?

This chapter will show readers how to avoid common errors and conduct productive appraisals. Readers will learn how to analyze employee performance prior to the appraisal and conduct structured

interviews using specific climate-setting techniques to involve em-
ployees, effective feedback to describe employees' performance,
questions and probes to solicit commitment from employees, asser-
tion skills to present unpleasant information, and behavioral strate-
gies to cope with difficult behaviours.

John stared hesitantly at the stack of papers on the corner of his
desk. It had been a pretty good month so far but he knew the joy
ride was almost over. He had put off conducting performance appraisals as long as he could.

When the forms had been distributed three months ago, John was
in the midst of a new project. His boss had let him off the hook to
get the bid out. The following month he had attended two major
conferences and hadn't had time to meet with his staff. He didn't
really have a good excuse last month, but his boss had been too
busy to track down the appraisal forms. Now, John had no choice.
The Vice President of Human Resources had called this morning
and explained the situation in terms that few people could mistake.
"Get them done this week or we'll find someone who can." And then,
just to add insult to injury, she added, "and be sure you do them right
the first time this year."

John grimaced as he recalled the problems he had last year. He
wanted to make sure that his people got good raises and he had
rated them all "outstanding." He had even talked to several of them
before his boss called him in to explain the company's philosophy:
"Nobody is perfect—never rate someone outstanding because then
you don't have any leverage when you need to make changes."

John's situation is a little more extreme than most. However, almost everyone who works with managers hears a number of stories
like it. Ask any group of managers what they like least about their

You can't imagine how much anger and frustration is caused by our
performance evaluation system. My boss acts like everyone else is
responsible for making it work. He climbs all over me if I'm even a
day late, but he hasn't given me an appraisal in the last five years.
Worse yet, he's always yelling at me to get tough, but the last time
one of my people complained he folded under the pressure and left
me hanging. You can be sure I won't let that happen again.
—A frustrated manager

job. There is a good chance that performance appraisal will be near the top of the list. When they talk about performance appraisals, managers complain that they don't like "playing god," passing judgments, or making real people fit an arbitrary curve.

The fact that performance appraisals are so unpopular is complicated by the fact that they are used in so many places. Studies show that more than 90 percent of all commercial organizations use some form of performance appraisal. In addition to business organizations, all federal and state government agencies and most local governments use performance appraisals. Moreover, the percentage without appraisal systems appears to be declining every year.

This situation gives rise to an interesting question. If performance appraisals are so unpopular, why are they used in the overwhelming majority of organizations? Studies show that appraisals are used for a number of purposes. The most common reason is providing a basis for compensation. Other reasons include building a foundation for improved performance, providing feedback, documenting performance problems, establishing guidelines for promotion, identifying training needs, selecting candidates for transfer, justifying discharges and layoffs, conducting personnel research, validating selection procedures, and providing a foundation for manpower planning.

Most organizations use performance appraisals for several purposes. Most managers mention several when they are asked about the performance appraisal system. The important thing to note is that it would be difficult to find any one system that could do all of the things on the list, even in the best of times. When you add the fact that both employees and their managers are uncomfortable with the performance appraisal process you can easily see why there are problems.

Common Problems

Researchers have identified a number of recurring errors. Although we don't need to use their vocabulary, it may help to mark out the most common problems.

The first problem is known as a *leniency* error. This means that many managers rate their people higher than statistical estimates say they should. For example, one group of managers consistently rated their people "outstanding" while statistical estimates predicted that no more than one in five should be placed that high. Another group placed ninety percent of their subordinates in the top 3 percent category. Many organizations have reported similar patterns.

Some managers say that leniency isn't really a problem. "All of my people are in the top 5 or 10 percent," they say, "because I wouldn't have anyone else working for me." That may be true but it overlooks some of the principal reasons for conducting appraisals. If you plan to use performance appraisal to select candidates for promotion and unusually large raises, it doesn't help if everyone is rated at the top of the pile.

Central tendency is the second problem researchers have identified. They have found that many managers tend to avoid giving "extreme" ratings. For example, some appraisal forms use a five point scale beginning with "needs improvement" and working up through "satisfactory," "average," "good," and "outstanding." A manager might avoid using both "needs improvement" and "outstanding," instead rating everyone as "average" or "good."

Again, you need to understand why central tendency is a problem. It is almost impossible to select people for promotion, training, or transfer if they all have similar performance ratings. Worse yet, some companies have found themselves in legal trouble when they tried to fire unsatisfactory employees. This has been a real problem when the employees were members of minority groups or were in other legally protected classes. Even though their managers knew the employees were not working up to standards, the courts have interpreted ratings literally. In effect, the courts have said that you don't fire someone because their work is "satisfactory" or "average." When employees in protected classes are involved, many courts have concluded that the companies were engaging in illegal discrimination.

The final problem with performance appraisals is called a *halo error*. This is the term used whenever a manager bases the evaluation of a subordinate on one or two things instead of looking at all parts of the subordinate's job. For example, secretaries are usually expected to schedule appointments, type correspondence, answer phone calls, greet visitors, sort mail, maintain filing systems, and keep track of supplies. If a secretary does an unusually good job of scheduling and managing correspondence, the boss may be inclined to overlook problems in other areas. Halo errors can also have a negative effect. If a secretary made a serious blunder in scheduling appointments, the boss might overlook real skills in other areas.

Halo errors also create problems because they make it impossible for the appraisal system to do what is expected. For example, you can't do an effective job of manpower planning when you can't count on the ratings of important skill areas. Similar problems arise when you try to develop training programs or test selection procedures.

Avoiding the Problems

You can see why leniency, central tendency, and halo errors are all serious problems. Alone or in combination, they make appraisal systems unreliable; many experienced managers know you cannot depend on them. Is it any wonder that most managers don't take appraisal too seriously?

Few, if any, aspects of management reveal as disappointing a gap between potential and actuality as does performance appraisal. Under certain conditions, performance appraisal can contribute to . . . laudable goals . . . [But] those "certain conditions" are seldom created. To make matters worse, many organizations act as if they were unaware of them.
—Saul W. Gellerman, *The Management of Human Resources* (Dryden, Illinois: The Dryden Press, 1976), p. 165.

Teachers, researchers, and practitioners have all tried to overcome these problems. Teaching managers how to measure subordinate performance has been one common approach. Training in filling out the appraisal form has been another common approach. Some carefully controlled studies have combined both approaches. Researchers have even taken managers on week-long retreats to discuss problems with appraisal systems and develop measurement and rating skills.

Most of these efforts have accomplished very little. Although some had good effects initially, their results seemed to disappear or wash out as soon as the managers got back to their old jobs. That finding is instructive because it points to two important conclusions.

First, few managers need to be trained to measure subordinate performance. Training may be a good thing, but most managers know who is doing well and who isn't.

Second, training in filling out appraisal forms really misses the point. Of course, life gets easier for secretaries and others if all of the appraisal forms are filled out the same way. But that is about all such training accomplishes.

What most managers need is help in discussing performance with their subordinates. Of course, it is easier to talk to some subordinates than to others. But the fundamental problem remains: It is hard to discuss performance when you don't have the skills required to give effective feedback. The sidebar on this page lists the greatest concerns voiced by managers in one study.

MANAGERS' CONCERNS IN CONDUCTING PERFORMANCE APPRAISAL INTERVIEWS

1. Maintaining a good working relationship with someone while criticizing the person's performance
2. Dealing with anger and confrontation
3. Being forced to justify negative evaluation
4. Being unable to show that evaluations are fair and objective
5. Lacking resources to reward superior performers

Audiences for Performance Appraisal

Thinking about appraisal as a communication process focuses attention on an important element—the audience. In almost every kind of communication, the audience, the person you are talking to, is the most important factor. That is as true of performance appraisal as of any other kind of communication. Let's look at some typical members of your audience.

Sally Whitehat is every manager's dream. Talented and cooperative, she has a long track record of success. Her performance has always been at the top of the pile. She willingly takes on new assignments and can really be counted on "when the chips are down." She is easy to get along with, generally anxious to please, and seldom has a bad word to say about anyone.

Joe Danger is like Sally in some ways, but you never know quite what to expect of him. He also has a long track record of success and his performance is generally good. The problem is that he has never been particularly friendly and you really have to watch him. He acts like he can do anything, but you always have the feeling that he is out to get you. Although he can be friendly when he has to be, you have never been particularly comfortable with him and like to keep him at arm's length.

Steve Good-old-boy is one of the friendliest and most cooperative employees in your shop. He always has a good word for you, and you always enjoy running into him socially. Lately, however, his performance has really slipped. Now you know that you have to keep an eye on him because he has bungled a couple of major projects and doesn't seem to be doing anything to solve his personal problems.

Karl Rotten is the one employee you really wish would go away. His work is spotty, at best, and he has a generally sour disposition. He seldom admits to creating problems and willingly points the finger of blame at others. You used to try to talk to him about his work and attitudes, but he pretty much told you to mind your own business and you still haven't figured out what to do with him.

Mary Newkid is your youngest employee. With you less than a year, she is still finding her way. Her work is OK and she is generally easy to get along with. You don't see her very often because she tends to keep to herself. Her work hasn't caused any problems but she hasn't done anything to distinguish herself either.

Of course your employees have different names, but there is a good chance you recognize some of the same types in your shop. In fact, these stereotypes are based on fairly extensive research, and most managers have—or know—at least one employee in each of these categories. Let's look at them a little more systematically.

Sally Whitehat seems like the perfect employee. She probably is, and it is easy to see what distinguishes her. Her performance is good *and* she maintains a good relationship with her boss. Joe Danger is also a good performer, but his relationship with the boss is strained. This relationship makes him seem untrustworthy, and some managers feel threatened by his presence. Steve Good-old-boy is friendly and easygoing. He maintains a good relationship with his boss but his performance is less than satisfactory. Karl Rotten combines all the bad features of the others. His work is substandard and he has a poor relationship with the boss. In most organizations, he is a candidate for termination. Finally, Mary Newkid is really sitting on the fence. Her work is acceptable but undistinguished, and she hasn't really established a relationship with her boss.

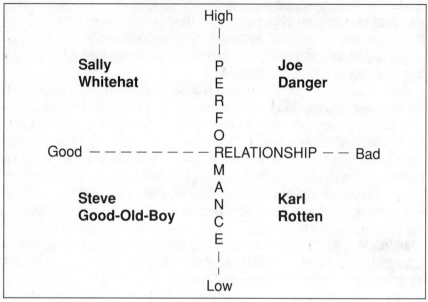

Figure 4.1   Audiences for performance appraisal

If we were to put these five employees in a diagram, it would look like the one in Figure 4.1. It is hard to show Mary Newkid on this diagram because she is right in the middle. Her performance is neither high nor low, and her relationship to the boss is neither good nor bad. As you will see in the next section, she is the one subordi-nate over whom you may have the most influence.

Appraisal Strategies

Classifying your employees as we have is an important first step in preparing to conduct appraisal interviews. Each of the employees represents a distinct problem and you will want to approach each of them in a different way.

It is hard to think of Sally Whitehat as a problem. Her work is good and she has a positive relationship with the boss. Unfortunately, some managers make a real error when meeting her for an appraisal interview. Because she is so productive and cooperative, most man-agers are anxious to help her grow. Consequently, many feel that they can really level with her. The result is often disastrous. In their desire to help her grow, these managers drag out long lists of faults and errors. Of course they want to help, but the results can be destructive. In fact, some studies show that managers present Sally with more pure criticism than any other employee. The result is long and painful interviews, and—in some cases—deteriorating relationships.

You can avoid this problem by thinking about what you would like to accomplish in the appraisal interview. You probably want Sally to continue to perform in an outstanding way and to maintain a good relationship with her. "More of the same" may not sound like an exciting objective, but I would settle for it.

Now the important question is how can you conduct the interview to give yourself the best chance of fulfilling the objective. I think your best chance is to be open with Sally. Explain that you are pleased with her performance and the relationship you have established, and then briefly cover the main points of the interview. We'll see what those points are in a minute, but it is important to understand why I say "briefly cover" the main points.

If there is any tension in the interview, there is a real chance that things you say may be misinterpreted. Moreover, you probably don't need to spend a great deal of time with Sally because chances are good that you spend a good deal of time with her anyway. That means that issues that you might need to discuss with other subordinates are usually dealt with in your daily interactions with Sally. You don't want to make her feel slighted—if anyone deserves your attention, she does—but there is no reason to prolong the interview. Short, sweet, and to the point is your best strategy. If there are things she would like to discuss, let her take the lead. But remember, there is no reason to make this interview a major event.

It is easier to see what the problem will be in interviewing Joe Danger. Because your relationship is strained, he may feel that you are not giving him full credit for his performance. And, if you feel threatened by him, there is a real chance that you are not being fully objective.

Again, think about what you would like to accomplish. In the best of all possible worlds, you would like to encourage continued outstanding performance and you would like your relationship to improve. However, we don't live in an ideal world and you would be wise to settle for continued performance. You can live with a distant, professional relationship as long as Joe knows you will not punish him for not being your best friend.

This situation calls for a particular strategy. This is an interview you conduct "by the numbers." In other words, the form of this interview is as important as the content. Use the system you have been given; be fair, thorough, and objective. It is particularly important to make sure Joe knows you are minding the shop and both the feedback and criticism models presented later in this chapter will help you present an appropriate image.

Low Perf + Rel

Appraising Steve Good-old-boy creates a unique problem because he may try to use his relationship with you to defray criticism of his performance. Even when he doesn't mention your relationship, he is likely to remind you of the time you have worked together, accomplishments from his past, and he may even introduce personal problems as a means of distracting you.

This may be one of the most painful interviews you ever conduct. Again, think about what you would like to accomplish. You would like to maintain the relationship while addressing performance problems in a way that will help Steve correct them. The tough thing about this interview is that Steve may not let you focus on performance. In extreme cases, he may even hold the relationship hostage. He will convey an attitude saying "if you are really my friend, you won't give me a bad time." The unfortunate thing is that giving him a bad time may be the only way to get your job done.

The strategy guide for this interview is easier to describe than execute. You need to be fair, firm, and focused. Fair in recognizing his past accomplishments, firm in evaluating current performance, and focused on the performance issues. Time and again, he will try to distract you by calling attention to your relationship. And, time and again, you will need to direct attention back to the performance questions.

Low Perf - Rel

Appraising the Karl Rottens of the world probably causes managers to lose more sleep than anything else. Lost sleep, elevated blood pressure, and extreme anxiety are all symptoms of a manager preparing to appraise Karl.

The fact that your relationship with Karl is poor means that you probably don't spend a great deal of time with him between appraisals. As a result, the interview may seem very much like an annual ritual in which you are both called upon to atone for your sins. You know that the interview will not be pleasant. He will probably come prepared to blame you for all the problems he has encountered during the past year. And both of you know that little positive is likely to come from the session.

Sound familiar? If you say "no," you are luckier than most managers. Almost all managers encounter a Karl at some point in their careers. The important thing to remember is that you have little to lose in conducting the interview. What is the worst thing that could happen? He may well lose his temper. He may even get so mad that he threatens to quit. What would you do if he actually carried out the threat? Most managers would celebrate!

The fact that you would be better off if he quit is the key to your strategy. Of course, you would like him to straighten out, but that is unlikely. It is most probable that you are really developing documentation to justify a termination action. That means you need to come prepared for a verbal dogfight. This has to be an interview that you control. He is most likely to interpret problem-solving efforts as signs of weakness that he will exploit. Your attitude should say, "We are not here for a conversation. Your performance is unsatisfactory and I'm here to tell you what needs to happen for you to keep your job." This also means that you need to be well prepared for this interview. Be sure that you have supporting documentation for the problems you will point out, and be sure that you have the support of your manager and of the Human Relations or Personnel Department.

Mary Newkid is the last one of the typical interviewees. In this case, there is no clearly defined pattern; she is right in the middle. Neither relationship nor performance are problems. And neither are particular assets.

Although the fact that she has not distinguished herself may be frustrating, it also means that you have a fairly good chance of influencing her behavior. She can become a good performer or a poor performer, and your relationship with her can be positive and supportive or negative and destructive. Your conduct toward her may be the determining factor.

Strategically, you ought to treat her like what you want her to become. Researchers have documented self-fulfilling prophecies in so many studies that there is little doubt that they can shape the behavior of your subordinates. If you want Mary to become another Sally Whitehat, you need to treat her like Sally. That means you need to treat her as if she already were an outstanding performer with whom you have a good relationship. You may need to spend a little more time to explain your procedures to her than to Sally. And you may have to go out of your way to spend time with her outside the appraisal interview. But that extra time can have a powerful effect on her future, and most managers would conclude it was worth the investment.

Providing Feedback

"Feedback" is a term that was popularized by systems thinkers following the Second World War. They used it to refer to information from one part of a system returned to another for the purpose of monitoring or changing performance. For example, a thermostat can be called the feedback element of a heating system. When the system works properly, the temperature registered by the thermostat is used to adjust the output of a furnace.

Social scientists use the term in much the same way. When we talk about feedback in performance appraisal, we mean information from a manager to a subordinate for the purpose of adjusting behavior. For example, a manager may expect a saleswoman to average seven calls a day. At the end of a week the saleswoman might report that she had made eight calls on Monday, five calls on Tuesday, six calls on Wednesday, eight calls on Thursday, and only two calls on Friday. That is an average of just under six calls per day. The saleswoman is close to the expectation but still can make some improvement.

If her manager provides the feedback in an appropriate way, we can expect the saleswoman to adjust her behavior. That is, we would expect her to increase the number of calls she makes by about one a day.

The only problem is that the saleswoman might actually decrease

---

An effective feedback process lets followers know how well they are doing the job on a regular basis. It is unrealistic to expect followers to improve performance if they are unaware that performance problems exist. People should know that they are being evaluated on a regular basis before their formal periodic evaluation occurs. Many performance problems can be caused by a lack of necessary coaching and performance feedback.
—Paul Hersey and Kenneth H. Blanchard, *Management of Organizational Behavior*, 5th ed. (Englewood Cliffs, New Jersey: Prentice-Hall, 1988), p. 370.

the number of calls she makes if the feedback is delivered in an inappropriate manner. In fact, we know that feedback can have very negative results when it is given in a harsh, uncaring way. Any time information is presented in a way that makes the persons receiving it feel that they need to protect themselves, it is likely to be destructive.

When we feel threatened psychologically, we normally react by throwing up barriers against the threat. This type of response is what is referred to as a *defensive reaction*. Once that defense reaction occurs, effective communication is drastically curtailed. Frequently, our messages are constructed in such a manner as to pose some degree of psychological threat to the receiver. Thus, it is worthwhile to learn of those message characteristics that may contribute to the arousing of defensive postures.
—Jerry W. Koehler, Karl W. E. Anatol, and Ronald L. Applbaum, *Organizational Communication* (New York: Holt, Rinehart and Winston, 1981), p. 70.

In practical terms, this means that the way feedback is communicated is often as important as its content. Look at the two samples below:

John, in the last week you have been late to work three times. On Tuesday you arrived at 8:15; on Thursday you got in at 9:45; and on Friday you came in at 8:27.

John, I've just about had it with you. You are never here on time and I just don't think I can count on you. Unless you shape up, I'm going to have to replace you.

The important thing to note is that both messages could be used to respond to the same behavior. If you really wanted to get someone's attention, the second is sure to do it. However, as feedback, the second example has far less information and may trigger a defensive reaction. It is easy to anticipate the subordinate responding, "You really have it in for me, don't you? Go ahead and replace me if you think you can!"

Obviously, if getting rid of the subordinate is what you want to accomplish, you may choose the second approach. On the other hand, if you really want the subordinate to change behavior, you have a much better chance using the first.

Researchers studying the way people respond to feedback have isolated seven characteristics that are associated with effective feedback. Let's take a look at each.

First, effective feedback is given in private. This is easy to understand because nobody likes to be embarrassed in front of friends and coworkers. Even when the feedback is positive, some people may be embarrassed to receive it in a public way.

Second, effective feedback is balanced. This means that effective feedback includes both positive and negative elements. Feedback is effective only when the manager recognizes both good and bad behaviors.

Third, effective feedback is relevant. In other words, you need to provide feedback about things under the person's control. It doesn't do any good either to blame or praise them for things over which they have little control.

Fourth, effective feedback focuses on specific behaviors. In fact, the more specific the information, the more likely you are to influence the person's behavior. Look again at the two samples above. Telling a person that he was late three of five days and providing detailed information about the days and times not only shows that you are paying attention, it also gives the person a clear sense of your expectations. Saying that someone is "never here on time" is both untrue and so damning that the person may never recover.

Fifth, effective feedback is based on knowledge. To be able to guide someone, you need to know what the appropriate standards or expectations are. For example, telling data entry persons that they need to work harder shows that you are unhappy with them but doesn't establish a clear expectation. In contrast, telling them that they are averaging 5,000 keystrokes per hour while the generally accepted standard is 12,000 keystrokes per hour provides clear guidelines. And if you can go the next step in telling them how to increase their performance you may have made a real contribution to their growth.

Sixth, effective feedback is personal. This is an important point to remember because there is a natural tendency to avoid unpleasantness by saying, "I'm not giving you a bad time, it's just the way the system works." Of course the system may set standards, but you are the system and your relationship to the subordinate may be more important than any set of standards. Most people work for you, not for the system. They will grow and develop as long as they feel they have a personal relationship with you. Once they need to worry about an impersonal system, they are more likely simply to withdraw or find other ways to protect themselves.

Finally, effective feedback is presented without judgment. This may be the hardest one of the seven principles to follow. Most of us wouldn't be providing feedback unless we had made a judgment, either good or bad. Again, the way you communicate the feedback is at least as important as the content. In the two examples above, the first is clearly less judgmental than the second. The first provides specific information that describes the person's behavior while the second only presents the judgments of the manager.

Coping with Criticism

Few people like to hear criticism. As managers we are no different. One of the most difficult things about conducting appraisals is that our subordinates may end up criticizing us. And, like it or not, there are often times when we should hear the criticism. Listening may provide information we need in order to grow. Listening may also help our subordinates feel more comfortable in the appraisal process. And opening the appraisal to a two-way flow of information is likely to make it more personal and productive.

The problem is that few of us know how to respond to criticism. Our natural instincts are to avoid it. When we can't get away, we are likely to deny that we have done anything wrong, find excuses, or strike back. None of these are productive responses.

The following model shows you how to listen to criticism without accepting blame or striking back.

Step one: Listen attentively. Make sure you understand the criticism. You may even paraphrase the other person's remarks.

Step two: Ask for details. Find out as much as you can about the incident or incidents described. You may ask a series of questions like these:
Who was involved?
What happened?
When did it happen?

Where did it happen?
How did it affect you?
Why do you feel it was improper?

Step three: Find something to agree with. You don't need to admit
that you were wrong but it doesn't hurt if you really were. More
important, you need to acknowledge the person's right to criticize
and to recognize the importance of the person's concerns.

Responding to Difficult Behaviors

There is one other skill you need to have in hand when you conduct performance appraisals. Some of your employees are likely to
respond with behaviors that most of us find difficult. These are behaviors that may throw us off guard and make it hard to stick with
our agendas.

You probably encountered most of the typical forms in the first few
appraisals you conducted. Some employees may try to avoid being
criticized by blaming their coworkers. "I know the project was a flop,
but it wasn't my fault; so-and-so never got his share done," is a
common response. Other employees will try to avoid criticism by
questioning the fairness of the appraisal system. They may say
things like, "It really doesn't matter because I don't have a fair chance
anyway." Still other employees will question your motives. "You are
really out to get me, aren't you?" or "You never wanted to hire me
in the first place, did you?"

Another response is to ask how you rated other employees. "Did
you mark Sara down as much?" or "I bet you weren't as hard on
Carol, were you?" Finally, some employees become silent and unre-
sponsive or they agree with everything you say. In either case, you
can tell that they really aren't listening to you, they are just agreeing
to get the appraisal done as quickly as possible.

As you can see, these employees have a pretty good set of tools
for throwing you off stride. They won't always use them, but
whenever they feel pressured, you can bet they will pull out one or
more of these techniques.

These responses are often hard to deal with because they are
unexpected. Many of us are inclined to ask, "What's wrong with him?
Why did he do that to me?" The answer is "Nothing is wrong with
him. He got exactly what he wanted—he distracted you and took
control of the appraisal." To counter these threats, you need to have

a set of tools for dealing with them. Here is one approach that works for many managers.

Step one: Listen to the subordinate; make sure you understand what he or she is saying.

Step two: Decide whether the behavior is really a difficult behavior (one designed to distract you) or an expression of a legitimate concern. If it is a legitimate concern, deal with it now or schedule another time to get back to it. If it is simply a difficult behavior, go on to step three.

Step three: Restate your purpose and get back to your agenda. For example, if someone tried to distract you by blaming coworkers, you might say, "I realize that other people had some difficulties and I am dealing with them as well. But, right now, I want to discuss your work."

You may need to use this approach several times. However, if the difficult behavior persists, go on to step four.

Step four: Call attention to the difficult behavior. You might do it this way: "John, it seems like you are trying to blame everyone else. I get the feeling that you are trying to avoid discussion of your work."

This four-step process is often effective. You may find other approaches, and you may need to keep refining your approach because some people will keep finding new ways to catch you off guard. Whenever that happens, make a mental note to work out a solution and get back to the business at hand, conducting the appraisal interview.

Conducting the Interview

Conducting the interview may be the easiest step in the process. If you have taken time to analyze your audience, develop an interview strategy, and think through the kind of feedback you want to provide, you are free to concentrate on communicating with the other person. Actually, being able to focus attention on the other person is critical. The performance appraisal interview is one of the most important forms of communication any manager ever directs.

Set the tone for the interview by scheduling it well in advance.

Performance appraisal is an important part of your job and it is important for your subordinate as well. By setting a definite schedule, you keep yourself on top of the process and alert your subordinates to the importance of the event. And, by scheduling the interview well in advance, you encourage the interviewee to participate in the process.

Appraisal discussions are personal, and you should choose a private location. Avoid interruptions and ask your receptionist to hold all nonemergency calls.

As you saw in our discussion of appraisal strategies, some interviews take longer than others. I suggest you pick a convenient mean and schedule each interview for an hour. You can always finish early or extend the interview if you need additional time.

Plan to discuss six distinct topics with each interviewee: the individual's job, standards by which performance is evaluated, current levels of performance, plans for improvement, support that you or the company can provide, and long-term prospects. You may face a minor problem with this agenda: Most appraisal forms do not include all these topics or follow this order. You can get around this problem if you remember that the communication process is far more important than sticking to the form. Give the subordinate a draft of the form a day or two before the interview and refer to it whenever you want. But follow an order with which you and the interviewee are comfortable, regardless of the form employed by your company.

Begin the interview with a casual greeting and quickly summarize the appraisal process. You probably understand the process better than most of your employees, and they may appreciate seeing it in context. At the end of the introduction, list the topics you want to discuss and move quickly into the first.

Interviews will be more effective if interviewees feel that they are active participants in the process. Allow them to say as much as they want about each topic and be sure to acknowledge their input. In fact, avoid coming to the interview with a finished form because few subordinates will participate actively if they see that the evaluation has already been completed. "Why bother," they ask, "when the boss has already made up his mind?"

After you have discussed all six topics, summarize the items on which you have agreed. And, give the employee one more chance for input by asking, "Is there anything else we should discuss?"

With the close of the interview, there are two more items to agree on: set a time for the interviewee to sign the finished form, and schedule opportunities for future discussion. Some employees will not need a formal schedule—you see them frequently anyway. Other employees may need a definite schedule. Setting a schedule is especially important if the employee is trying to overcome specific performance problems. You may go to the extreme of setting weekly or even daily times for brief meetings, just to see how things are going.

Conclusion

Although few managers are fond of performance appraisal systems, almost all organizations insist on regular appraisals of all employees. Appraisals are used to provide feedback, to help employees grow and develop, and to satisfy legal requirements governing employment actions.

Appraisal systems are powerful management tools, but many managers make leniency errors, central tendency errors, and halo errors. These problems can be avoided by developing skills needed to conduct effective appraisals. These skills include identifying the audience, selecting a strategy, providing feedback, coping with criticism, responding to difficult behaviors, and conducting the interview. The John Smith case following this chapter shows the importance of each of these skills.

Suggested Readings

Bernardin, H. John, and Richard W. Beatty. *Performance Appraisal: Assessing Human Behavior at Work.* Boston: Kent Publishing Company, 1984.

Bramson, Robert M. *Coping with Difficult People.* New York: Ballantine Books, 1981.

DeVries, David L., Ann M. Morrison, Sandra L. Shullman, and Michael L. Gerlach. *Performance Appraisal on the Line.* New York: John Wiley & Sons, 1981.

Ewing, David W., ed. *Harvard Business Review: Performance Appraisal.* Cambridge, Massachusetts: Harvard College, n.d.

Kellog, Marion S. *What to Do about Performance Appraisal.* Rev. ed. New York: AMACOM, 1975.

Kirkpatrick, Donald L. *How to Improve Performance Through Appraisal and Coaching.* New York: AMACOM, 1982.

Latham, G. P., and K. N. Wexley. *Increasing Productivity Through Performance Appraisal.* Reading, Massachusetts: Addison-Wesley Publishing Company, 1981.

Mairer, Norman R. F. *The Appraisal Interview.* New York: John Wiley & Sons, 1958.

Morrisey, George L. *Appraisal and Development Through Objectives and Results.* Reading, Massachusetts: Addison-Wesley Publishing Company, 1972.

Case Study:
John Smith

John is a 24-year-old engineer nearing the end of his second year at Slimpickings, Inc. This is his first job since graduating from a first-class university. His academic credentials are excellent: 3.96 GPA; Dean's List seven semesters; scholarship support during his junior and senior years.

John's starting salary was 25 percent above the average. Although he was hired by Mark Johnson's predecessor, he has worked for Mark his entire time at Slimpickings. This is his third appraisal conducted by Mark. His six-month probationary appraisal rating was "excellent" and he has continued on a fast track. At the end of his first year, he was again rated "excellent" and has been given some project management responsibilities as a result.

At present, John is assigned to provide technical support for three major projects and is the Lead Engineer on two smaller projects. His technical support work continues to be outstanding. Everyone who works with him on those projects talks about his reliability, innovativeness, and ability to meet deadlines.

John has excelled at technical support, but his salary is considerably higher than the norm for someone in a technical support role. Mark has been able to justify the unusual salary by pointing to John's academic credentials and his growing role as Lead Engineer. However, Mark's supervisor is concerned about the size of the salary differential and has begun exerting pressure for Mark to move John into a more fully developed managerial role.

Mark had assigned John the Lead Engineer role as a way of easing him into managerial assignments. Unfortunately, there have been some problems on the projects and several people have blamed John. He has built a reputation as an arrogant bully, and few clerical or support people are willing to work with him. He is frequently curt when giving instructions and usually blames staff or support people when things don't get done properly. He has been working extraordinarily long hours—65 to 75 hours a week—for the last couple of months. When asked, he says that he is trying to get things back on track and complains about the incompetent staff he has to work with. His normally short fuse has gotten shorter.

Mark is more than a little uncomfortable about conducting the appraisal interview. While John's technical support work remains outstanding, Mark believes he is responsible for problems on the two projects. At the very least he is sure that John is not delegating effectively, and he has growing reservations about John's interpersonal skills.

Mark has attempted to discuss the situation with John, but John repeatedly blames the problem on other people. Mark has asked John to enroll in a management development workshop sponsored by Slimpickings, but John has refused. He "hasn't been able to find the time," he says, and he doesn't intend to try because the problems are "not my fault, anyway."

Recently, there have been a number of rumors that John is looking for another job. He has been openly critical of Mark's management style, and Mark is beginning to feel that things would be better if John moved on. In fact, John has become something of an embarrassment to him and Mark knows he needs to turn the situation around soon. John's technical skills are excellent, and he clearly has the potential to become a good manager. However, his resistance to learning interpersonal skills has compromised their relationship and made it difficult for Mark to discuss the ongoing problems with him.

Largely as a result of their strained relationship, Mark hasn't told John that customer representatives for both of his projects have begun to complain. Both are concerned about missed deadlines. And both report that John has been abrupt and impolite when asked about the situation.

Mark has reviewed both projects and found them to be roughly 6 months behind on 36-month schedules. By themselves, these delays would be minor concerns. However, Mark cannot allow things to get further behind, and he is upset by John's unwillingness to accept responsibility.

Mark has prepared the following form to guide the appraisal but is unsure how to approach John.

ANNUAL APPRAISAL FORM
SLIMPICKINGS, INC.

EMPLOYEE: *John Smith*
SUPERVISOR: *Mark Johnson*

RATING*	ACTIVITY	COMMENTS
5	Technical Knowledge	John clearly understands the projects to which he is assigned and actively conducts appropriate research. He reads current journals and appears to be abreast of recent developments affecting his work.
4	Analytical Skills	John is a skilled problem solver in technical areas. This rating is lower than last year and reflects his inability or unwillingness to apply the same skills to dealing with customers, staff members, and clerical employees.
3.5	Initiative	Again, John is outstanding in technical areas. However, he shows resistance to developing interpersonal skills and has not attended five management development workshops for which he has been nominated.
3.5	Dependability	In support roles, John's performance has been outstanding. However, both projects for which he has lead responsibility are behind schedule and both customers are dissatisfied. I have attempted to discuss timelines with him but have not seen appropriate progress.
3	Management Potential	I believe John has a great deal of potential. He has been targeted for promotion and assigned lead roles to develop his skills. Unfortunately, neither project is moving smoothly and John has not learned to delegate work to others.
3.5	Overall Evaluation	While John is technically strong, he has not developed needed interpersonal or managerial skills.

* 5 = Outstanding performance
  4 = Above average performance
  3 = Average performance
  2 = Below average performance
  1 = Performance significantly below average

Mark's evaluation appears to be colored by interpersonal factors. What would you like to accomplish if you were conducting the appraisal? Would you use the form presented? What changes would you make? How would you present the bad news to John?

5

Interpersonal Negotiation and Influence

Today's managers seldom have enough authority to get their jobs done. New ways of structuring organizations—for example, project and matrix structures—have reduced managers' ability to control scarce resources. The same factors of production are assigned to several managers at once and they are left to work it out. Is it any wonder that office politics can make or break a manager's career? In addition, employees no longer respond to orders—they expect managers to reason with them. Employees with sought-after skills can cut their own deal and simply bail out when unhappy.

Working with people over whom they have little direct control has forced managers to negotiate with superiors, coworkers, and subordinates. Unfortunately, many have adopted traditional hard bargaining strategies. Often the only model managers know, hard bargaining was developed as a means of dealing with labor unions and other outsiders. Characterized by threats and counterthreats, hard bargaining aims to wear down opponents as skilled negotiators try to get as much as they can.

While still appropriate for dealing with some outsiders, hard bargaining causes problems when used for interpersonal negotiation within an organization. Agreements reached through hard bargaining

141

are always unstable: Winners constantly try for more while losers work to get back what they lost.

Today's managers need a new approach to negotiation, an approach that produces stable agreements—agreements that both parties want to preserve. This chapter will introduce a positive approach to interpersonal negotiation.

Readers will learn to establish a climate of trust and promote mutual problem solving. They will learn to listen to the needs of the other party and to use questions and probes to establish a common agenda. Using assertion skills to describe their needs, readers will learn to focus on common problems while setting aside personal attacks that interfere with the problem-solving process.

Opportunities to Negotiate

Negotiation is all around us. It fills our personal and professional lives. Negotiation is such a commonplace activity that we often overlook opportunities to develop and polish our skills.

Let's look at some common examples.

Stacey is the leading salesperson in her division and has established a reputation as a "territory-builder." After eighteen months of hard work, she has gotten established in her current territory and is reluctant to move again. Unfortunately, the company is experiencing unexpected competition from a new firm in another region. Bob, the division sales manager, is concerned and would like Stacey to move so the company can "meet the competition head on."

Mark is planning to buy a new car. He has spent several weeks studying his choices and has settled on the model he wants. There are three dealers in the area that carry the model, and Mark has decided to approach each to see where he can get the best deal. The salesman at the first lot realized that Mark was prepared to go elsewhere and promised the "best deal in town" if Mark is prepared to buy today.

Clyde, Eric, and John are repairmen for a computer services company. Their work involves quite a bit of driving from customer to customer. It is not unusual for each of them to drive 45,000 miles a year. Even though their trucks are serviced regularly, the trucks wear out faster than the company replaces them. Delivery of a new truck often causes controversy and the crew supervisor, Cynthia, has complained that deciding who gets a new truck is a no-win situation for her. When a new truck arrived, she called Clyde, Eric, and John in for a meeting and told them to work it out.

Pat and Marsha have been dating for a little over a year. They have gotten into the habit of going out for a casual dinner on Fridays followed by a relaxed evening watching television. Pat enjoys these quiet evenings, but Marsha has been pushing to do something "more exciting."

Dawn is the owner of a secretarial service providing temporary help for local businesses. She treats her 21 employees like members of her own family, she says, and was surprised to learn that they had formed a union. Less than a week after the union was recognized, Dawn received a certified letter demanding higher wages, increased benefits, and more predictable employment.

These examples are typical of negotiations that fill our personal and professional lives. Looking at them again will help to make two important points about negotiation.

First, negotiation always involves two or more parties. Each party can be a person, as in most of our examples, or a group of people, as in the union confronting Dawn.

Second, people find themselves in negotiation because there is a conflict—apparent or real—in their interests. Stacey would like to stay where she is while her manager wants her to move. Mark wants to keep looking for the best deal, but the salesman would like him to sign a contract right away. Clyde, Eric, and John all want the new truck. Pat wants a quiet evening at home while Marsha wants to do something more exciting. And Dawn would like things to stay the way they are while her employees want increased salaries, greater benefits, and more predictable work schedules.

Managing these conflicts of interest is the heart of negotiation. The important thing to note is that any relationship may give rise to conflicts of interest. This is important because recent changes in the way we do business have focused renewed attention on three kinds of relationship that create new opportunities for negotiation.

New Opportunities for Negotiation

One of the most dramatic changes in the way we do business results from the importance of skilled workers in high-tech environments. In traditional assembly-line manufacturing operations, for example, workers were required to have relatively few skills. Replacements could be hired easily and slipped into the line with little need to teach them specialized skills. Workers were hired for their hands, it was said, not for their heads.

Under these circumstances, workers found strength in unions. Any one employee could be easily replaced, but the whole crew could not be—especially when they resorted to strikes and picket lines. Confronted with unions capable of closing their facilities, managers quickly developed hard bargaining techniques. They learned to offer as little as possible, made concessions only when absolutely necessary, and sought to enforce the letter of the law in interpreting contracts.

The development of high-tech industries requiring skilled employees has changed management's relationship to labor in some fundamental ways. Strength in numbers is no longer a critical bargaining tool, and the rapid decline in union membership in recent years tells a large part of the story. Instead, employees have strength in the knowledge and skills that make it possible for them to do jobs few other people can. Finding replacements for skilled workers is no longer easy. In fact, growing labor shortages indicate that things may get worse before they get better.

The growing importance of skilled employees increases their value to organizations. Skilled workers are in such demand in some fields that they may simply bail out when dissatisfied. In fact, competitors may be anxious to hire them because of the knowledge and experience they bring.

Under these circumstances, techniques developed to deal with groups of employees protected by unions are no longer appropriate. Managers should seek to forge lasting, stable relationships with each employee. And, because employees are individuals, each must be dealt with on his or her own terms. Standardized benefit packages may appeal to some groups of employees, but for different reasons. One employee may value the health care, another may focus on the retirement plan, and still another may be interested only in take-home pay. As a result, managers may find themselves negotiating with employees on a one-to-one basis.

The development of new work structures is a second factor creating new opportunities for negotiation. In traditional organizations, each manager had sole control over a set of resources. These resources included employees that worked for the manager alone, physical space and equipment that no other group used, and raw materials earmarked for that specific unit.

Business has learned much from politics. But until now, business has ignored one of the most potent tools in the political game—the power persuasion tactics used by lobbyists, politicians, and other interest groups to *get what they want*. In the one-on-one world of the owner-managed business, decision-making was clear-cut, if not always agreeable: You presented your idea to the boss, and either he said yes or he said no. The answer usually depended on whether your vision matched his, and perhaps on whether he liked you or not.

Those days are long gone. Power today means much more than having the boss's ear. In the complex and fragmented world of conglomerates and high corporate turnover, power has taken on subtler meanings. Like politics, it is often a give-and-take game in which players must call their shots and go after only the most important—or most attainable—stakes. Decisions are usually made by several people in power and often depend on many hidden factors. Power today requires a blend of managerial talent, psychological instinct, and persuasive charisma. Effective executives on their way to the top know this and must constantly decide which decisions are the crucial ones. They also need to build alliances and coalitions to get their ideas—and themselves—across.

—William D. Coplin and Michael K. O'Leary, with Carole Gould, *Power Persuasion* (Reading, Massachusetts: Addison-Wesley Publishing Company, 1985), p. ix.

This ownership of resources made management a relatively simple task. Whenever a machine was needed, it was there waiting to be used. Similarly, employees, plants, and raw materials were set aside and generally available when needed. There was no need to negotiate agreements or to schedule around other users.

While ownership made management relatively simple, it also increased costs and reduced efficiency. Specialized resources owned by one manager often went unused. For example, drafting equipment might be used only during design phases of a project and then warehoused until needed again. At the same time, other groups might also own their own drafting equipment, which was also stored much of the time.

Organizational design experts recognized these inefficiencies and set about finding ways to eliminate them. Project management structures and matrix organizations are two of the most common results.

Under these schemes, individual managers do not own many resources. Instead, the resources are owned in common by a group
of managers, and each must negotiate with the others or with a
central office to make sure the resources are available when needed.

For example, one design engineer might be assigned to work on
five or six separate projects. He reports to (is "owned by") a functional manager, but actually works for five or six project managers.
His time is a scarce and valuable resource. The project managers
working with the functional manager must decide how best to use
the engineer. Success or failure of each project may depend on the
project manager's negotiating skills.

The final change in the way we do business involves changing
relationships with vendors. American firms have traditionally avoided
long-term relationships with their suppliers. Each major purchase
has been treated as a separate event and potential suppliers asked
to bid on each contract. Management often awarded contracts to the
lowest bidder, regardless of any ongoing relationship.

This strategy had some short-term benefits, but it also created
adversarial relationships. With everyone trying to cut costs to a
minimum, vendors had little interest in the quality of the materials
they supplied; they simply met the specs and let the buyer beware.

Today, growing numbers of firms recognize the value of establishing long-term relationships with their suppliers. For the buyer, these
relationships can yield higher productivity, better access to resources, and significant competitive advantages. Vendors also
benefit from stable relationships because they are able to guarantee
employment for their workers. They can also concentrate on improved product quality, careful inventory control, and innovative
designs.

Long-term relationships with suppliers benefit both parties, but
they also call for very different approaches to negotiation. Traditional
bid-purchase approaches are no longer appropriate. Instead, representatives of both firms engage in negotiations to establish relationships, identify common interests, explore values and limitations of
different contract provisions, and develop means of dealing with con-
tingencies. Moreover, as both parties develop an interest in maintaining the relationship, they lose their freedom to "cut and run" when
problems develop.

These changes—the growing importance of skilled employees,
organizational systems for sharing resources, and the desire to

establish long-term relationships with suppliers and customers—increase opportunities for negotiation. They also require the use of negotiation strategies and tactics unlike those used in traditional settings. To understand these strategies and tactics, let's look at some typical approaches to conflict.

Approaches to Conflict

One way of dealing with conflict is simply to ignore it. Someone using this style is said to withdraw. People may resort to this style because they hope the conflict will simply go away. For example, Stacey, the salesperson in our first example at the start of the chapter, might simply ignore her manager's requests to discuss a new assignment.

A second approach to conflict is to try to get what you want at the other party's expense. People who adopt this strategy are known as tough battlers. They use everything they can put their hands on to make sure they get what they want—no matter how much it hurts the other party. Books on negotiation frequently list the tricks of the trade that are designed to force the other party to go along.

Negotiators playing "hard ball" have developed many tactics designed to give themselves an advantage. Some of the most common tricks are listed here.

Some negotiators drag out the negotiation process and introduce their most serious demands after the other party is emotionally exhausted.

Another common trick consists of making new demands when the other party thinks the negotiation is almost concluded.

The physical setting in a room may be controlled to make the other person uncomfortable and anxious to settle quickly.

Making excessive demands is another common ploy. Negotiators using this tactic hope that a compromise will work to their advantage because they have asked for far more than they really expect.

Finally, negotiators may develop a smoke screen by focusing attention on minor points and hoping that the other party will let major concerns pass unnoticed.

In the examples above, Clyde might decide that he should get the new truck because he is the senior man. To force Eric and John to go along, he might try to threaten or intimidate them, and he probably would sabotage efforts to find other solutions.

Sacrificing your own interests to make the other party happy is a third approach to conflict. Someone responding this way gives up whatever they must to satisfy the other person. People using this strategy are often called friendly helpers, and it is easy to see why. For example, Pat might decide that making Marsha happy is so important that he gives up a quiet evening, buys tickets to a rock concert, and invites a group of friends to go with them.

Compromise is a fourth approach to dealing with conflict. Someone using this approach usually acts as if they were cutting a pie into pieces. They try to be as fair as possible, and they often go to great lengths to make sure everybody involved gets the same amount. For example, Dawn might respond to her employees' demands by saying that she can't afford to guarantee them work ("no" to demand number three) but she can give them a small raise and pay half the cost of a medical insurance policy ("fair" responses to demands one and two).

The final response to conflict is known as problem solving. Someone using this approach treats conflict as a problem to be solved. They try to find a solution that satisfies everybody's interests. For example, Stacey might suggest that she stay in her own territory but spend a couple of days a month helping another salesperson open the new territory. Mark might offer to sign a contract giving him a refund if another dealer advertises a better price in the next three months. Clyde, Eric, and John might agree to get rid of the worst truck first and then find a way to distribute the remaining trucks. Pat might volunteer to take Marsha somewhere special on Saturday if she lets him relax on Fridays, and Dawn might agree to her employees' demands if they can help her increase business volume to cover the extra costs.

Values and Limitations

Many people talk as if problem solving is the only approach a person should use. So called win-win strategies have been described in many books and articles, and there have been many seminars teaching people how to use these strategies.

Of course, win-win strategies are attractive, but they aren't always the best approach. In fact, each of the five strategies has unique values and limitations.

Withdrawing is an appropriate strategy when you simply don't care what happens. In fact, it may be the best strategy to use when someone else is trying to involve you in a fight that doesn't make any difference to you.

Although withdrawing is appropriate in some cases, there are limitations. When you withdraw from a conflict, you lose the ability to influence the outcome. Moreover, you not only sacrifice your interests, you miss the opportunity to strengthen your relationship with the other party.

In popular literature, tough battlers are often portrayed as being heartless, cruel, and selfish. Some of these descriptions are accurate, but that shouldn't obscure the fact that there are times when this style is appropriate. Tough battlers come into their own in two special cases.

First, if the other party approaches negotiation as a tough battler, using a similar strategy may be your only choice. People who withdraw, help, solve problems, and even those who seek compromise may get eaten alive by tough battlers. In the extreme, tough battlers use all the power and influence at their disposal to get their way. They play on their opponents' weaknesses, resort to threats and intimidation, and do whatever they can to prevent more reasonable people from determining the outcome of negotiations. Faced with such an opponent, you have little chance to do anything else.

The second case in which it makes sense to be a tough battler arises when you aren't concerned about maintaining a relationship with the other party. Although we don't often think about these cases, there are some that show up every day. Buying or selling a home is a common example.

Being a friendly helper is appropriate whenever you value building and maintaining a relationship more than any specific interest being discussed. This is especially important in service industries, and some innovative firms have put satisfying customers above all other concerns. Some even provide unconditional service guarantees promising to satisfy the customer, no matter what it costs.

Compromise is also an appropriate strategy in some circumstances. Of course the disadvantage is that neither party gets everything they want. This means that the relationship may be unstable as both parties try to get more next time. However, compromise has the advantage of being relatively quick, especially when both parties will be satisfied with a quick and dirty solution.

For example, a marketing program from which two program managers get roughly equal benefits can be paid for on a 50/50 basis. At the same time, there may be very sophisticated ways of finding out who benefits most and it would be possible to devise payment systems to reflect differences in value. But when all is said and done, measuring the value of the program and devising a formula to distribute the costs would probably take more time than it is worth. Under these circumstances, compromise is probably the best solution.

Problem solving is the last of the five strategies. In many respects, problem solving is the best strategy because it maximizes both interests and relationships. When used properly, both parties get all of what they want *and* they strengthen their relationship.

Although problem solving is the most desirable solution, it also demands the greatest commitment from the participants. Properly done, problem solving will consume more time than any other approach. The parties need time to explore their mutual interests and to develop innovative solutions.

In addition to time, problem solving also requires the most of another scarce commodity—*trust!* Effective problem solving requires a climate in which both parties can freely explain their needs and concerns. Any hint that either party is being less than honest in stating their needs will destroy the necessary climate. Worse yet,

---

AVOID SHOWDOWNS

Somehow, negotiating has become confused with machismo, as though the whole point is to outlast your opponent, to make him back down first.

The point of negotiation is to reach an agreement that is mutually advantageous to both parties. To make it a contest of egos can only work against you. Don't use phrases like "deal breaker," "take it or leave it," or "that's nonnegotiable"—anything that makes you sound like you're daring the other person to knock a chip off your shoulder.
—Mark H. McCormack, *What They Don't Teach You at Harvard Business School* (Toronto: Bantam Books, 1984), p. 148.

---

any suggestion that either party will abuse the problem-solving approach to take advantage of the other—in this negotiation or in future cases—will poison the relationship.

Understanding these approaches to conflict and the way they affect negotiation is essential background information. Skilled negotiators use this background to analyze situations and select approaches that fit each. Now it's time to look at a general approach to negotiation built on this background.

An Approach to Negotiation

The opening pages of this chapter have shown you why negotiation can be so complicated. No matter how simple a problem appears to be, the presence of another party forces you to be conscious of quite a few variables. As you approach negotiation, you need to think about the nature of the problem or conflict. You also need to think about your interests, about the things you would like to accomplish.

You also need to understand how the other party is likely to respond to the situation. This can be relatively easy when you know the other people involved. However, even long-time friends and associates can surprise you when the stakes are big enough. And when you don't know the other players, you need to be prepared to deal with all five approaches to conflict.

There can be so many factors involved in a negotiation that it is hard to design a single procedure that will cover all cases. The easiest approach is to divide the process into three general stages: activities before the negotiation session, conduct during the negotiation session, and concluding the session. Even understanding these stages is not enough. Negotiation can be derailed at any point and you need some tools to keep the process on track. These tools are commonly called tactics. We will look at some of the most important ones following our discussion of the negotiation process.

Before the Negotiation Session

Much of the hard work involved in negotiation should be started before you attempt to resolve the conflict. In fact, several things have to happen before you even recognize the need to negotiate.

Conflict is a recurrent feature in our daily lives. As you saw above, our days can be filled with conflicts. Some of these conflicts are minor annoyances that you probably choose to forget about. For example, it doesn't make much sense to pursue a driver who cuts you off in traffic. Other conflicts have more meaningful or lasting consequences. And some conflicts call up such strong emotional reactions that it would be difficult to avoid dealing with them.

All of these conflicts are more often felt than understood or acknowledged. The feeling that something is not right is a sure sign of conflict. Before you can engage in negotiation, you need to define the conflict as precisely as possible. It has been argued that definition is unnecessary in routine business negotiations, but I disagree. Even when negotiation seems routine, taking time to define the underlying conflict will help you identify assumptions that would otherwise limit your flexibility and put you at a disadvantage.

Begin by acknowledging the conflict and trying to identify the situations or events that created the need to negotiate. As you examine the situation, you may find it useful to ask yourself five questions:

> Why am I reacting so strongly?
> What would I like to get out of this situation?
> How will I do it?
> What are my alternatives?
> How is the other person likely to respond?

These are commonsense questions, but they represent fundamental elements of any conflict situation. The first question directs attention to your emotions and to the assumptions you have made about the situation. Exploring these features will help you evaluate the importance of the conflict and alert you to assumptions that may need to be checked out before going further.

For example, it is easy to dismiss some conflicts at this stage. The driver who cuts you off in heavy traffic is a case in point. As you look at your reactions you may realize that the situation isn't really very important—the other driver didn't really take something from you. And you may recognize a faulty assumption—"I ought to do something about that clown." This is when you decide whether or not the conflict is worth pursuing. Remember, negotiation can be time-consuming and some conflicts may just not be worth the time and effort required to solve them.

The second and third questions—"What would I like to get out of this situation?" and "How will I do it?"—call attention to your interests and positions. Your interests are the things you value or need, while positions are approaches to securing your interests. You can think of positions as bargaining chips, things you are willing to give up to get what's really important to you.

The difference between interests and positions is so important that you need to be comfortable with the distinction. Let's take a moment to look at an example. Suppose you are shopping for a new car. Your interests, the things you absolutely need, are economical transportation for you and your family, a high degree of reliability, and a feeling of safety. Of course dealers could satisfy these interests in several ways. One might propose to upgrade a relatively inexpensive import. Starting with a price under $10,000 he could add an extended warranty, air conditioning, an advanced stereo system, and so forth, bringing the price up to $16,500. If you begin arguing about price at this point, you are locked into bargaining over positions. Look carefully and you will see that some features of the position—the air conditioning and stereo—are unrelated to your interests.

In this example you can see the danger in bargaining over positions. If you spend all your time haggling over price, you may never consider other alternatives that might serve your interests. For example, a low mileage, two-year-old station wagon selling for $11,500 may be a better buy if you can also get an extended warranty.

Exploring your alternatives, the object of the fourth question, is a way of deciding how much effort to invest in negotiation. Begin with the assumption that it is always possible to develop a negotiated agreement to any dispute. However, it will be more difficult in some cases than others. If you have few alternatives and the situation is important, then it may be worth investing a great deal of effort in finding a negotiated agreement. On the other hand, if you have many alternatives to a negotiated agreement, you may simply go elsewhere.

Return to the car dealer problem for a minute. The dealer has proposed to sell you an upgraded economy car at an inflated price. If you must buy a car quickly and there are no other places to buy a car in the area, you may well be stuck dealing with him. In this situation you properly begin looking for ways to force his price down. Fortunately, it is very unusual to have so few alternatives. In this example, your alternatives include other dealers in the area, private parties selling cars through the newspaper, and you may even find a way to rely on public transportation for a while.

The important point is that your alternatives set the boundaries for negotiation. When you have few attractive alternatives, you need to negotiate and may even be forced to make some concessions. However, you need to be less committed to negotiations when you have even one attractive alternative. It may be time to walk away when your alternative is more attractive than the negotiated agreement.

Finally, you need to prepare yourself for the other party's reactions. The more you can learn about the other party, the better your chance of controlling the outcome of the negotiation.

When you know the other party, you may already know enough to prepare yourself. If you don't know them, you may need to do some research. In either case, you should be able to make some judgments about their interests and positions, their alternatives, and their customary ways of dealing with conflict.

Think about some of the situations you may expect to encounter. You know you are in for a difficult time when the situation is more important to you than to the other party, the other party usually responds to conflict as a tough battler, and you have few alternatives. On the other hand, you may approach the negotiation far differently when the situation is equally important to both of you, there are few alternatives to a negotiated agreement, and both of you prefer to respond to conflict as problem solvers.

Once you have done your homework, it is time to meet the other party. Whenever I can use a problem-solving approach, I try to schedule a mutually convenient meeting in a setting where everyone will be comfortable. When problem solving is not an option, there are several things you can do to tip the balance of power in your favor. Common tactics include scheduling the meeting in your office or conference room, selecting a time of day when the other party is not at their peak, and arranging seating to your advantage, perhaps with the sun shining in the other party's eyes. These can all be effective tactics, but most sophisticated people know how to counter them. Worse yet, if you begin with a tactic designed to give yourself advantage, you should expect the other person to react in ways that preclude problem-solving approaches.

Conduct During the Negotiation Session

When you meet the other party, it is probably a good idea to get down to business fairly quickly. Prepare a mental agenda with the following steps:

1. briefly introduce the problem
2. secure agreement on the problem
3. search for alternatives
4. select the best alternative

This is an idealized agenda and there are a number of places where things can go wrong. The other party may respond in ways that make it impossible for you to follow through, and the negotiation may break down at any point. However, you have your best chance of success if you are prepared for each step in advance. And if you have considered your alternatives, you know when to pack your bags and walk away from the negotiation.

Let's look at each step in the process. In the next sections we will discuss some tactics you can use to control the situation.

Step One: Stating the Problem

A quick greeting and a few social pleasantries may help create a comfortable atmosphere, but you don't want to delay too long. The longer it takes you to get around to your reason for calling the meeting, the greater the chance the other party will get defensive.

We all have our own personal style, and you should use an approach with which you are comfortable. Many experienced negotiators prefer to begin with a simple statement of the problem, as they see it. For example, you might use the following introduction to begin a meeting with a coworker.

> Good morning, Steve. Thanks for joining me. Let me tell you what I wanted to talk about.
> With the new organization in place, we both use the same mailroom facilities. I have a big job ready to go out on the fifth and I happened to see that you have a job scheduled to go out at the same time. I'm not sure that the mailroom can handle both jobs at once and I wanted to see how we can work around the bottleneck.

This introduction is pretty simple and straightforward. It explains the problem in neutral terms and suggests an approach to the situation: *We* should find a way to work around the problem. The use of "we" suggests a problem-solving approach and you should notice that there is no effort to assign blame. The meeting would be far different if someone began by saying, "You scheduled your job to interfere with my mailing" or "Now you've done it, how are you going to get us out of this mess?"

Step Two: Securing Agreement on the Problem

The other party's response to the introduction will tell you a good deal about them and about their approach to conflict. Some people will acknowledge the problem and move quickly to begin looking for solutions. This may be the best of all possible outcomes, and you would love to hear the other person say, "I see what you mean. Let's see what alternatives we can find."

Other people will respond by placing the blame on you or some third party: "That's not my problem; why don't you work it out with the mailroom?" And some people will take the problem personally: "Gee, I'm sorry. I'll postpone my job."

Any of these responses is possible and you need to listen carefully. You need to hear the other party's response to the problem—that is, their position—and you need to identify their response to the conflict situation. "It's your problem" signals a tough battler; "Gee, I'm sorry" marks a friendly helper; and "I wonder what we can do about it" probably indicates a problem solver or a compromiser.

Whatever the other party's reaction, you should be prepared to push ahead. For the negotiation to proceed, you need to get the other party to agree that a problem exists. Try paraphrasing their reaction to see if they agree that a problem exists. You might say something like "I understand your frustration because this has happened before. Do you agree that we should find a solution?"

You may need to try this step several times before the other party agrees. Don't be afraid to paraphrase their reactions several times if you need to. On the other hand, if the other party does not acknowledge a problem, you may need to conclude the negotiation and go to your best alternative.

Step Three: Creative Search for Alternatives

Once you have agreed that there is a problem, you may begin searching for alternatives. This is the time to be creative, and you may want to develop a number of possible solutions. Many people will suggest a solution and then begin debating its merits before looking for other possibilities. Try to discourage this by generating a list of alternative solutions before you start evaluating any of them. You might say something like this:

> John, I know we'll find a solution that will satisfy both of us. Let's see how many possibilities we can come up with before looking at any of them in detail.

If the other party agrees, start making a list and add to it until you have exhausted the possibilities. You may find that it is possible to list ten, fifteen, or even twenty solutions to most common problems. Most people make the error of stopping after they have listed only a few, but successful problem solvers expend a great deal of effort exploring possibilities.

Step Four: Selecting the Best Solution

Selecting the best solution is the final step in the process. By "best" we mean the solution that secures the interests of both parties. In some cases, you will be able to find solutions that give both people everything they want. That is the essence of problem solving. In other cases, one or two solutions will work to one person's advantage while the other solutions will favor the other person. Your attitude is particularly critical when you encounter this situation.

If you hold out for the one or two solutions that work primarily to your advantage, you reduce chances of finding a mutually acceptable solution. You may also poison your relationship with the other person. On the other hand, if you accept a solution that doesn't satisfy your interests, you have wasted a good deal of time without accomplishing much. Reviewing your alternatives to a negotiated agreement can help you decide what to choose.

If you have few attractive alternatives to a negotiated agreement, you may have to settle for any solution. If you have several attractive alternatives to a negotiated agreement, you may be wise to hold out for more. In either case, both parties should be satisfied with the negotiated agreement, and both parties need to feel that the negotiated agreement is better than they would have achieved without negotiation.

Concluding the Negotiation Session

Negotiation sessions always come to an end. Sometimes both parties have achieved their objectives and walk away satisfied. Other times, one or more participants feels a need for a break and plans to resume later. In other instances negotiations have reached a stalemate; someone decides it is not worth continuing.

The most difficult situation is the deadlocked negotiation. Both parties are locked into their positions and neither is willing to budge. Sometimes you can get back on track by using the tactics discussed in the next section. Sometimes you can't.

Negotiation is hopeless when the best agreement you can forge is less attractive than the alternatives. Traditional hard-line approaches would have you simply walk away when you reach this point. Walking away may be your best response if you will not need to deal with the other party again. However, we often use negotiation to smooth out differences in ongoing relationships. Walking away may not be your best approach if you will need to deal with the other party in the future. In fact, there may even be times when the relationship is so important that you are willing to sacrifice some of your immediate interests.

Of course, you don't want to give in all the time. Becoming a friendly helper would damage your stature and poison the relationship even more than failing to reach agreement. But you do need to give yourself and the other party a second chance. This may be a good time to focus attention on the relationship. You might say something like this:

> I'm really sorry we've reached this deadlock. We've solved so many problems in the past that I was sure we would be able to find a solution to this one.

With a little luck, a statement like this will get both parties back into a problem-solving mood. If not, try temporizing. Suggest a break so you can both develop some new perspectives.

> Wow, it seems like we're in a real deadlock here. I'd like to take a break and come back to this tomorrow. Is that OK with you?

Most people will bring new ideas or options when they come back to the negotiation. You may even be able to resume problem solving.

Unfortunately, there are some times when it is simply not possible to find a mutually acceptable solution. These are times when you fall back on your alternatives. No matter how frustrated you are, you need to close the negotiation with care and tact.

> Well, it looks like we aren't going to be able to find a solution this time. I'm sorry we couldn't work this one out, but I'm sure we'll have better luck next time.

Although this is a simple closing, there are two features you should be sure to note. First, the conclusion is phrased to avoid blaming either party. Nobody is at fault, *we* just couldn't find a solution. Second, failure is limited to this one occasion. We will be able to do better in the future. Both of these elements are important because they preserve the relationship between the parties. An ongoing relationship is preserved even though the parties couldn't solve this particular problem.

Tools of the Trade: Some Negotiation Tactics

Reaching a satisfactory conclusion depends on the problem-solving skills of the negotiators and their ability to control the negotiation. Several popular books describe negotiation tactics designed to give one party an advantage over the other. The tactics described here are designed to help both parties control the negotiation for their mutual advantage. These are powerful tactics and you should be prepared to use them again and again throughout any negotiation.

Tactic One: Focusing on the Problem

Focusing attention on the problem is particularly important when you are dealing with someone who uses blame or other diversionary tactics. For example, the other party might respond to the mailroom problem by saying, "You are always interfering with my work. Why don't you leave me alone so I can get my job done?" This is a tough response because two elements are present: diversion and blame. You can respond by focusing on the problem: "John, the problem we have to deal with is the two jobs hitting the mailroom on the same day. Let's see if we can find a way out of this spot."

Tactic Two: Limiting the Scope of the Problem

Limiting the scope of the problem is a second tactic. Like the first, it is particularly useful when the other party employs diversionary tactics. "You never give me a fair shake" and "I always have to do it your way" are two of the phrases you may hear in interpersonal negotiations. In more formal business situations, you may hear diversionary tactics that may include things like references to prior deals or unrelated concerns.

Whenever you encounter diversionary reactions, you can keep the negotiation moving by focusing on specific elements of the current problem. Get away from terms like "never" and "always" by pointing to elements of the present negotiation. "What would you consider fair in this situation?" and "What would you like to do in this situation?" may focus attention on the immediate concern.

You may also use this tactic when the other party presents you with a laundry list of concerns. This is a common diversionary tactic and you need to be prepared to deal with it. For example, the other party may respond to your concerns by listing all of the problems they have faced. You may never get anything done if you try to respond to all of their concerns. Instead, focus on the specific problem; your approach should be one of solving problems one at a time.

Tactic Three: Search for Common Interests

As you saw above, it is often important to distinguish between your interests and your positions. Interests are the things that you want to accomplish while positions are more like the chips you bargain with.

Distinguishing between interests and positions may also help you keep a negotiation on track. Identifying interests shared by both parties may help you to find common ground and reduce haggling over positions.

For example, two account executives struggling to get work out through the mailroom may both want top priority. In practice, that means they both want their jobs to go first.

"My job first" is a position that may disguise common interests. If the two account executives step back from their positions, they may find common interests that outweigh their personal motives. Serving particular clients or getting materials to critical customers may be common interests that make it possible to resolve the conflict.

Tactic Four: Emphasize Areas of Agreement

Negotiations occasionally break down when they are on the verge of reaching agreement. This often happens when one or both parties are so concerned about the differences in their positions that they fail to see the amount of progress that has already been made. It is not uncommon for rival negotiators to become so fixed on the differences that divide them that they fail to recognize the number of issues that have already been resolved.

Summarizing areas of agreement is one useful way to keep a negotiation on track. For example, negotiators in a recent labor dispute had worked for several days to resolve seventeen points of contention. With fifteen already resolved, the two negotiators locked horns over the sixteenth issue, and it appeared that the negotiations were deadlocked. Fortunately, one of the participants recognized the danger and was able to prevent a total breakdown by merely summarizing the points that had already been settled. His remarks are worth quoting:

> When we began four days ago we disagreed on seventeen major items. We are now down to two points. The items on which we are in agreement include salary levels, additional benefits for new employees, and a uniform grievance procedure. With all that behind us, don't you think we can find a way to resolve the last two issues?

This tactic can be used again and again. The more strained the negotiation and the more tension the parties feel, the more important it is to recognize what they have already accomplished.

A Closing Note: Power and Politics in Organizations

Throughout this chapter, we have talked about negotiation without referring to a pair of closely related topics: power and politics. This was deliberate because the words themselves often sound dirty or unethical. For example, we say, "He got the promotion, not because he was talented, but because he played politics" or "She doesn't have a lot of ability, but she sure has some powerful friends."

These criticisms may be true but they tend to obscure an important point: power and politics are inevitable in every organization. That is a sweeping generalization, and you may find a case or two that seem to be exceptions. Before making too much of the exceptions, consider the following.

Organizations are designed to deal with routine kinds of problems. As long as nothing out of the ordinary happens, the normal processes deal with things in a routine way. However, when something unexpected happens, the normal processes don't seem to fit. Think about some of the situations that may not be covered by normal processes: a key executive resigns unexpectedly, a junior employee develops a promising new product, a critical client threatens to take their business elsewhere, a trusted employee is arrested for work-related conduct, or a government agency announces an investigation into the company's business practices.

These are exceptional circumstances and the normal procedures just don't work.

In these cases, organizations need to find novel responses. This almost always means going outside the accepted system. This is when power and politics become most apparent. Major decisions are made by members of the old boys network while other members of the organization feel bypassed or "submarined."

Much as you may be angered by the use of power and political games, you need to see what is happening. Because the normal processes don't cover exceptional cases, key decision makers find it necessary to rely on personal relationships. These relationships make it possible for organizations to muddle through.

Far from being new or temporary, these personal relationships have been built over years of interpersonal negotiation. Although they may not be needed in the normal course of business, these relationships are vital resources in times of crisis.

Some people emerge as major players in times of crisis. They wield substantial power and influence the course of organizational politics because they have carefully built relationships through normal day in and day out negotiations. Power and politics are not games reserved for a few. They are open to everyone who negotiates with an eye to building and maintaining relationships.

Conclusion

This chapter has focused on negotiation. It began by noting that we are surrounded by opportunities to negotiate and that a number of changes have increased opportunities for professional negotiation. These changes include the growing importance of skilled workers, increasing use of nontraditional organizational structures, and efforts to improve competitiveness by building ongoing relationships with vendors. Collectively, these changes call for new approaches to negotiation.

In the most general terms, negotiation is an effort to resolve conflicts, and the way a person approaches conflict often determines the outcome of negotiation. Common approaches include withdrawing, tough battling, helping an opponent, compromising, and problem solving. Each of these approaches has values and limitations, but problem solving is most likely to produce long-lasting agreements.

Although there are many variations, a general approach to negotiation includes three phases: analysis before entering into the process, problem-solving strategies during the process, and means for reaching a conclusion. Tactics—the tools of the trade—include focusing on the problem, limiting the scope of controversy, searching for common interests, and emphasizing areas of agreement.

A closing note looked at power and politics in organizations.

The cases following this chapter give you a chance to practice your approach to negotiation. In the first, a manager is confronted with a demanding but talented subordinate who has lost confidence in him and made an "end run" to his superiors. In the second, a manager is faced with the need to negotiate relationships with her peers and a key subordinate. There are a number of distractions in both cases and your first step should be distinguishing between positions and interests.

Suggested Readings

Anthony, William P. *Managing Your Boss*. New York: AMACOM, 1983.

Bolton, Robert. *People Skills*. Englewood Cliffs, New Jersey: Prentice-Hall, 1979.

Cialdini, Robert B. *Influence*. New York: William Morrow and Company, 1984.

Coplin, William D., and Michael K. O'Leary. *Power Persuasion*. Reading, Massachusetts: Addison-Wesley Publishing Company, 1985.

Fisher, Roger, and Scott Brown. *Getting Together*. Boston: Houghton Mifflin Company, 1988.

Fisher, Roger, and William Ury. *Getting to Yes*. Boston: Houghton Mifflin Company, 1981.

Hart, Christopher W. L. "The Power of Unconditional Service Guarantees." *Harvard Business Review* (July–August 1988): 54–62.

Jandt, Fred E. *Win-Win Negotiation*. New York: John Wiley & Sons, 1985.

Karras, Garry. *Negotiate to Close*. New York: Simon and Schuster, 1985.

Laborde, Genie Z. *Influencing With Integrity*. Palo Alto: California: Science and Behavior Books, 1983.

LeBoeuf, Michael. *How to Win Customers and Keep Them for Life*. New York: G. P. Putnam's Sons, 1987.

Mackay, Harvey. *Swim With the Sharks*. New York: William Morrow and Company, 1988.

McCormack, Mark H. *What They Don't Teach You at Harvard Business School*. Toronto: Bantam Books, 1984.

Nierenberg, Gerard I. *The Complete Negotiator*. New York: Nierenberg & Aeif Publishers, 1986.

Schatz, Kenneth, and Linda Schatz. *Managing by Influence*. Englewood Cliffs, New Jersey: Prentice-Hall, 1986.

Spekman, Robert. "Strategic Supplier Selection: Towards an Understanding of Long-Term Buyer-Seller Relationships." *Business Horizons* (August 1988): 75–81.

Case Studies:
Jane Doe

Jane is the only female employee in your department. She has just received a promotion, and you expect her to receive another in the next few months. You are very pleased with her work and have regularly acknowledged her contributions to your group's efforts. In fact, you have asked her to attend the senior staff meeting with you several times. Attending the senior staff meeting is important recognition because it gives her the opportunity to interact with your boss and to meet members of the next two levels of management. She is the only one of your subordinates you have invited to the staff meeting, and this has made her presence even more noticeable. Your boss's reaction has been very positive. He has complimented you on inviting Jane to the meetings, mentioned that he likes what he sees, and asked you to keep him informed about her progress.

Your relationship with Jane has been very positive for most of the two years she has worked for you. Unfortunately, things have begun to sour lately. Two months ago, she asked you to review her salary. She explained that several people in the lunchroom were comparing salaries. If what she heard was accurate, she was the lowest-paid employee at her grade and she didn't think it was fair. Moreover, since her divorce last year, it has been difficult to make ends meet, and her problems have been complicated by some unexpected medical expenses resulting from her oldest son's recent bicycle accident.

You promised Jane that you would look into the salary schedules and get back to her as soon as possible. Since that conversation, you have been tied up with several important projects including a couple for your boss. As a result, you have not been able to look into the salary question.

You have nearly finished a couple of projects and you plan to meet with Jane as soon as you get back from a conference with a major supplier. You had hoped to see Jane briefly on Tuesday before leaving but she called in sick so you simply left a note on her desk asking her to see you first thing on Monday.

Returning to work on Monday, you find two confidential envelopes on your desk. The first contains a memorandum from Personnel indicating that Jane has taken a two-week personal leave. The second contains a courtesy copy of a memorandum from Jane to your boss complaining about her salary. The memo lists several men doing similar work and notes that each is rumored to earn considerably more than she does. And, she notes, you had promised to look into the salary question but have done nothing about it.

What do you do now?

Hot Stuff Seafoods

Karen Anderson is one of five Regional Marketing Directors report-ing directly to Bob Masterson, Vice President of Marketing for Hot Stuff Seafoods, a national restaurant chain catering to upscale sea-food lovers. At 42, Karen is the youngest and considered by several insiders to be the most promising Director. She has been an out-standing success on all performance measures. Average sales, market share, and net return per facility in her region have grown by at least 20 percent per year during the last three years. Three of the other four regions have reported between 5 percent and 7 percent annual growth during this period. Only the eastern region has come close to matching her performance. Directed by Bill Taylor, Hot Stuff restaurants in the eastern region have reported growth between 13 percent and 17 percent on the same indicators.

Although Karen has tried to discourage rumors, she is frequently mentioned as the heir apparent for VP Marketing. Hot Stuff Seafoods has made it a practice to promote from within whenever possible, and Bill Taylor is the only other logical candidate. Age 52, Bill has never shown interest in the position, but he is known for playing close to the vest. Moreover, there is a substantial compensation differential between Regional Director and Vice President. It is un-likely that Bill would turn the position down if it were offered to him.

Several days prior to the monthly wrap meeting, Karen, the other Directors, and most of the staff noticed that Bob seemed unusually agitated. Never particularly comfortable around people, Bob had become even more reclusive than usual. He arrived before any-one else in the morning and stayed late in the evening. He avoided the cafeteria and ordered lunch and dinner delivered to his office. Kate Starr, his secretary, hired a temporary clerk to run errands while she guarded the entrance to Bob's office. When concerned Directors and staff began inquiring about Bob's health, Kate would say only that he was working on some "special projects." She re-fused to discuss the projects but reassured everyone that they were being done at the direction of Richard Dillon, founder, President, and CEO.

Tension was running high and all of the Directors arrived early for the month-end meeting. The agenda distributed three days prior to the meeting gave no clue to the events of the past week, and its blandness seemed to add to everyone's discomfort. Although he had always been punctual, Bob was nearly thirty minutes late. The delay added to the tension but no one spoke as Richard Dillon walked in with Bob. Dillon seldom attended division meetings, and his presence was a clear sign that something unusual was up.

Bob relinquished his customary seat at the head of the table to Richard and sat in the first chair on the left, a seat that had been quickly vacated by one of the Marketing Directors. Bob began the meeting by apologizing for the delay and thanking everyone for waiting. Then he announced that they would suspend the agenda to make way for a statement from the President.

Richard paused for several seconds and looked first at Bob and then at each of the Directors seated around the table. Karen felt her throat tightening, almost as if she were being strangled. She didn't realize it at the time, but Karen was one of the more composed people in the room.

When he finally began to speak, Richard traced the growth of Hot Stuff Seafoods from the hand cart he had bought as a boy just out of school. The Directors had heard the speech before, more times than they could count, but they still listened attentively. After twenty minutes of history, Richard paused briefly to catch his breath. He continued with the following remarks:

> Many people have contributed to the growth of Hot Stuff Seafoods, but none has contributed more than my close friend, Bob Masterson. Bob started as Director of Marketing when we could barely afford to pay the rent on our corporate headquarters. His help and guidance have been responsible for much of our success. He developed our first national marketing campaign, arranged our first celebrity golf tournament, and designed the administrative structure we use today. He also hired most of the people in this room.
>
> For many years, Bob has been one of the most important people at Hot Stuff Seafoods. Unfortunately, even the best of us get tired. Less than a week ago, Bob informed me he wanted to retire. I tried to talk him out of leaving us, but Bob convinced me that his reasons are sound and I have reluctantly agreed to let him go.

After a long pause, Richard continued.

> Bob has invested too much of his life in Hot Stuff Seafoods simply to walk away. He has agreed to stay with us for one more year. During

the next twelve months, Bob will be asking each of you to accept responsibilities that he has managed personally. During the transition period, the Board of Directors and I will consider our options and prepare for our next move. I ask each of you to continue to support Bob as you have in the past. In addition, my door is open to each and every one of you. I encourage you to come to me whenever you have concerns about the transition or ideas that you would like to share. Thank you all for attending!

With that conclusion, Richard stood, turned sharply on his heel, and left the room.

No one moved or spoke. At last, Bob broke the silence. "Thank you for joining us today. Ms. Starr will schedule appointments for each of you with me during the next week. I will see you then. We are adjourned."

Karen was stunned. The other Directors were visibly shaken—all except Bill Taylor. He sat calmly and confidently at the other side of the table—directly opposite Karen. He seemed composed, strangely unruffled, and he was the first to leave—without speaking to anyone. "Smug bastard," Karen thought. "I wonder what he knows that I don't."

Questions flashed through Karen's mind as she got up to leave. Was Bob fired? Why? What could he have done? And if he was fired, why are they keeping him on for a year? Who do I work for now? Bob or Richard? She hoped it was still Bob because she hardly knew Richard. She said "hello" to him at company functions, but that had been the extent of their conversations. Did he even know who she was? And why do Richard and the Board have to "consider our options?" Does that mean they don't plan to promote one of us? Or does that mean they plan to eliminate the position? Can they farm our work out to independent contractors? Where can I get another job? Do I even have a copy of my resumé? If Bob is really in trouble, who will write letters of recommendation for me?

Karen returned to her office, gathered up some correspondence and a couple of project reports, said good night to her secretary, and left for the weekend. She noticed that hers was not the first Director's car to leave the parking lot. Even Bill Taylor's new silver Mercedes had gone.

Monday began with a previously scheduled staff meeting. No one knew any more about the shake-up, and nobody talked about it. After the meeting, her secretary handed her a phone message ask-to see Bob Masterson, "at your earliest convenience." She walked slowly to his office wondering what was going to happen next.

Ms. Starr buzzed Bob when Karen got to his reception area. Bob came out of his office to greet her. He looked unusually tired for the first thing on Monday morning, but seemed cheerful and enthusiastic. Once in the office, he directed her to take a comfortable chair in his conversation corner. Sitting in the chair beside hers, Bob apologized for the abruptness of the phone message and the fact that he didn't have time for a cup of coffee with her. There were, he said, only a few minutes before he had to go to "another damn meeting."

Handing her a slim file folder, Bob spoke calmly and without emotion.

As you know, I have begun turning some of my work over to people who will be around after I am gone. This folder describes the start of a new media tracking program I have been developing. We want to know more about who sees our ads, how they respond to them, and what we can do to increase our "hit" ratio. This folder gives just the barest outline because I haven't had much time to get things off the ground.

Opening the folder, Karen found two sheets of paper. The first was a page photocopied from a textbook on business strategy. One sentence was underlined in red: "In today's competitive environment, organizations will survive by being more efficient than their competitors at every level of operation." Turning the sheet over, Karen found a hastily scribbled note suggesting that Bob spend some time finding out how they could increase the efficiency of their marketing. Commenting on Karen's successes of the last few years, the note also suggested she be given the project if Bob couldn't pursue it. The note was signed by Richard and dated from the previous month.

The second sheet was a copy of a memo from Bob to Bill Taylor. Dated that morning, the memo announced that "Karen Anderson has been given responsibility for the marketing efficiency study we discussed. Since her staff is already working at full capacity, please assign one of your people to work with her on an as-needed basis." Karen recognized Bill Taylor's handwriting in the response on the bottom of the page: "Chester is the only one of my people with any free time. I've told him to do what he can for her."

Before she could speak, Bob stood up and began walking toward the door. Grabbing his briefcase and glancing at his watch, he mumbled that he was late again, wished her well, and walked out.

Walking back to her office, Karen was aware of two emotions. She was angry about the way Bob had treated her, and she was determined to "show those bastards."

Once back in her office, Karen turned her thoughts to the task at hand. She had met Chester once or twice, but she knew him by reputation. In his early 30s, Chester was known to be "bright as hell, and almost as rebellious." People still told stories about the time he called a tow truck to remove the long black limousine blocking his parking space. Nobody was sure if he knew the limousine belonged to a visiting diplomat, but most figured he did. Only a quick-thinking security guard who refused to admit the tow truck prevented an international incident. Most people also knew that Chester had refused promotion in another division because the personnel officer was late for their appointment and didn't apologize. Karen was one of the few people who knew that the promotion carried with it a 20 percent raise amounting to almost $15,000 a year.

Chester also had a reputation for being unconventional. He lived with his wife and son in a 34-foot recreational vehicle because he "didn't like being tied down." An avid jogger, Chester frequently ran in marathons and often used vacations to attend seminars on health and fitness.

Most people wondered how Chester had lasted so long in the corporation. Karen wasn't sure, but she had a good idea. In spite of his resistance to authority and reluctance to commit himself to a conventional life-style, Chester had never failed to complete a project once he became involved. In fact, he often made his bosses look pretty good because he didn't seem to want credit for what he accomplished. Rumor had it that he saved Bill's group several hundred thousand dollars a year by watching for duplicate advertising spots. Media interested him, he said, and he kept track of things just to "see what would happen."

Glancing at the file one more time, Karen asked herself, what am I going to do about this mess?

6

The End of the Road: Managing Terminations

We live in a mobile society, and employment relationships change as often as personal relationships. Although this book has focused on establishing and maintaining good relationships with employees, managers also need to know how to bring an end to employment relationships.

Employment relationships end when an employee is terminated or when an employee voluntarily chooses to leave. In both cases, managers need to close the relationship in as positive a way as possible.

In this chapter, readers will learn to conduct termination interviews by (1) justifying the termination, (2) reviewing the termination decision with higher management, (3) communicating the termination decision, and (4) following up after communicating the decision.

Readers will also find vital information about exit interviews. They will learn why they should conduct exit interviews with employees who leave voluntarily, and they will learn how to schedule, conduct, and document the interview.

Growth and change are daily parts of our lives. Every day, we find ourselves in new situations and we learn new things about ourselves and our surroundings. The same is true of other people and of the organizations for which we work. Many of the challenges we described in the introduction—increasing competition, changing employee expectations, new working environments—are a direct result of these changes. And as the world around us changes, so does our relationship to the people with whom we work.

Personally and professionally, our lives are changing at a dramatic pace. Personally, we form new relationships, strengthen some existing relationships while allowing others to wither, and we may choose to discontinue some relationships.

Our professional lives often follow the same patterns. We hire some new employees and promote or transfer others. We watch as some employees retire or seek employment elsewhere. And we may take an active role in terminating other employees.

These changes in employment relationships are a natural consequence of our mobile, rapidly changing society. "Turnover" is the term we use to label changes in employee relationships. Like it or not, we know that turnover is inevitable.

Many firms have devised strategies to control or reduce turnover. Careful selection processes, detailed attention to working conditions and promotional opportunities, internal training and development, and exit interviews are just a few of the strategies employed. However, even the best-managed companies lose employees. Sometimes employees choose to move on because they find greater opportunities or more satisfying work elsewhere. Sometimes performance problems or other concerns make it necessary for management to terminate an employee. And sometimes the relationship loses value for both the employee and the company.

Although ending relationships is never easy, all indications are that it will happen more and more frequently in the future. Technological changes will render some plants and operations obsolete. Changing employee expectations will create demands that some firms cannot meet. And turbulence will create groups of employees who move from job to job just because change is exciting. As a result, managers at all levels need to be prepared to deal with employees who are leaving.

The important thing is understanding that the employee's relationship to the company and to the former manager may not end when the employment relationship ends. Whatever their reason for leaving, former employees may still have an impact on the company and their former managers.

Under the best of circumstances, former employees are potential customers, recruiters, and spokespeople for the company. They may also become competitors. When they do, their information about their former company can give them a substantial advantage over other competitors. Under the worst circumstances, former employees may use the legal system to attack their former employers. Both you and your company may be in jeopardy when a former employee files suit.

All of these outcomes are possible. The employee's last on-the-job contact with you can often determine what form the relationship will take after the employee leaves. Although it may not always be possible to part on good terms, what happens afterward is heavily influenced by the employee's feelings about you and about your organization.

In the best circumstances, former employees remember you favorably. One very sophisticated manager thinks of every former employee as a spokesperson of sorts. She says that running a department is just like running a public relations agency for the company.

> If I do my job right every former employee is a walking advertisement. I like them to tell our customers and other professionals what a fine organization we are. Even when we both agree that it is best for the employee to go elsewhere, I want them to carry away a positive impression.

In other circumstances, you may be able to reduce the damage when an employee leaves under less favorable circumstances. Here is how the same manager describes her attitude toward fired employees.

> It's never easy to fire someone. And I don't expect someone I canned to walk around singing our praises. But I would like them to feel that they learned something while they were here. And I would like them to accept at least some of the responsibility for being fired. That way, they are less likely to badmouth us in the future.

Finally, there are always legal reasons to treat former employees with care and dignity. Former employees can sue you and the company for the way they were treated while they worked for you. They can sue you for the way they were terminated. And they can sue you for things you say about them after they are gone.

Suits by former employees can cost hundreds of thousands of dollars—even when the company wins. And damage awards can run into the millions when the company loses. Worse yet, your former employees can sue you personally. Although suits against individual managers are less common than suits against companies, they are a possibility. There is even some reason to believe they will become more common.

As you have seen, your final contact with employees can have substantial impact on their subsequent behavior. When you fire an employee, the final contact is called a termination interview. When the employee chooses to leave, your final contact is called an exit interview. Both are important events in an ongoing relationship with an employee, and both should be conducted with care.

Termination Interviews

Employment law is a complicated field. It appears to become more confusing with every court decision, and there is no substitute for competent legal counsel when you find yourself involved in a job action. However, the central concepts are relatively easy to understand and may provide general guidance.

As you read this material, please remember that I am not an attorney and am not offering you legal advice. This book is no substitute for competent legal counsel, and you would be wise to seek counsel whenever you contemplate an action that may expose you to legal action. However, the materials in this chapter may reduce your risk of being sued and the amount of damage if you are.

"Employment at will" is a common law principle underlying most employment agreements in this country. Essentially it means that employment is a voluntary agreement between two parties: the employer and the employee. Either can terminate the agreement whenever they choose to. If there were no exceptions to the "at will" rule, you would be free to walk away from your job whenever you felt like it. By the same reasoning, your employer could fire you whenever it suited the company's purpose. Neither of you would have any obligation to the other following the termination.

Although the employment-at-will principle is easy to understand, there are several exceptions. These exceptions create situations in which you may not be free to fire an employee without legally defensible reasons. Most of the confusion in employment law arises from these exceptions. Questions may arise about whether they apply to particular situations, what kinds of obligations are created, and what penalty should be paid if you don't live up to your obligations. Although this is not intended to be a law book, understanding the nature of exceptions to the employment-at-will principle will help you recognize situations where you need to proceed with great care.

The first exception to the at-will doctrine applies to situations in which termination would be contrary to public policy. For example, an employee cannot be fired for reporting an employer who breaks the law. This exception is a factor in fewer cases than the others. However, it has been the dominant concern in a number of well-publicized whistle-blower cases.

The second exception to employment at will arises whenever a contract or implied agreement provides employees with some form of job security. For example, formal contracts often guarantee employment for a specific period of time.

Less formal agreements may also appear to provide employees with some measure of job security. Employment handbooks may describe an employee's first few months on the job as a "probationary period." Of course these provisions were intended to make it easy to fire unsatisfactory employees early in their tenure. However, the statements may also be interpreted to mean that an employee who gets through the probationary period has earned some measure of job security.

Employees who have secure jobs may be fired only when the employer demonstrates "good cause." This is a general term, and there can be a good deal of disagreement concerning its application to particular situations. Behavior that endangers life, violates regulations governing professional conduct, or violates significant company policies about which the employee was informed usually constitutes good cause.

The third exception is closely related to the second. Employees who have worked for a company for an extended period of time may be entitled to "good faith and fair dealing." This may be interpreted to mean that they cannot be fired arbitrarily. This exception is most important in dealing with employees who repeatedly commit minor infractions. Individually these errors would not constitute good cause for termination. However, a consistent pattern could be used to justify termination.

Although the pattern of errors could justify termination, most people assume that an employee should be given an opportunity to correct minor problems. In practice this means that you may need to document efforts to correct the employee's behavior. You might be required to show that (1) the employee's behavior is unacceptable, (2) the employee was aware of the problem, (3) you had given the employee a reasonable opportunity to solve the problem, and (4) the employee has not corrected the problem.

The final exception involves certain protected classes. Members of minority groups and others who have suffered discrimination in the past are protected by laws and orders designed to ensure equal opportunities. Employees in these groups can be terminated for good cause. However, you need to show that their performance is unsatisfactory. Here again, you need to document efforts to correct the problem and to show that you have dealt with the employee in a fair and equitable way.

As you can see, there are some formidable legal obstacles when you prepare to fire an employee. However, that does not mean that you should avoid taking the necessary action. If anything, these legal demands force you to think the termination action through to a logical conclusion and make sure that it is an appropriate action. Much of the work needs to be done prior to the termination meeting with the employee, and it may help you to divide the process into four steps: (1) justifying the termination, (2) consulting higher management and getting needed approvals, (3) communicating the message, and (4) action following the termination.

Step One: Justifying Termination

Termination should not be a spur-of-the-minute decision. You should never fire someone when you are angry or distracted by other problems. Instead, begin by taking time to think through the decision to fire.

Always take time to prepare a written description of the event or events that lead you to believe the person should be terminated. Even if none of the exceptions to the at-will doctrine apply, make sure you have good reason for termination. One way to do this is to prepare a written rationale describing your reasons for seeking termination. I know it seems like unnecessary work, but it has a number of advantages: it makes you take an objective look at the situation, it provides documentation for use in the next step, and it will provide a useful record should your decision be challenged in court or elsewhere.

Make your description as thorough and detailed as you can. Any event that figures in your decision should be described in some detail. The traditional journalists' questions may help you frame your thinking.

What happened?
When did it happen?
Where did it happen?
Who was involved?
Why was it improper?
How did it affect the company, other employees, the customers?

As you are preparing your rationale, review any documentation that is available. Reports of annual appraisals and any written warnings placed in the employee's file are important parts of the documentation.

Here you may encounter a particular problem. If the employee has been a trouble spot for some time but there is no documentation, you may not be able to justify termination. As you saw in the chapter on performance appraisals, courts may interpret appraisal reports literally. You may know that "average" and "satisfactory" ratings really mean that the employee is not doing an acceptable job. However, the courts may not share your view.

As a result, you may be stuck with an unsatisfactory employee for some time while you begin documenting the problem. You have to go back to square one: Show the employee that there is a problem, give a reasonable opportunity to correct the situation, and closely monitor progress. Careful documentation is essential at each step in the process.

Finding someone to talk to while preparing to terminate an employee can be particularly difficult. On the one hand, it often helps to get reactions from an impartial third party. On the other hand, you cannot afford to let the word get out. You may lose your ability to act if people think you are out to get an employee. Worse yet, you risk losing your credibility if your decision is overturned by higher management. If you aren't sure who you can trust, don't talk to anyone. Build your case and move on to step two.

Step Two: Reviewing the Decision
with Higher Management

Reviewing your decision with higher management is the second step. In some cases, this means discussing the decision with your immediate manager. Other firms have specific procedures designed to insure impartial reviews, and many organizations involve representatives of the Personnel Department.

This review is not intended to limit your authority, and you should not take it as questioning your ability to make a reasoned decision. Even when your company does not require a formal review of termination decisions, there are several important reasons for reviewing your decision.

Reviewing your decision with higher management is good business because it helps to insure objectivity. Performance problems can be extremely frustrating and your involvement may make it difficult for you to be impartial. Reviewing your decision with higher management helps to make sure you have not overlooked or misinterpreted critical information.

Review by higher management also guarantees that you have followed appropriate procedures, including those specified in contracts you may have never seen, and that your reactions are consistent with those of other managers. Both of these factors can be extremely important if your decision is challenged in court or elsewhere.

Higher management may also identify severance benefits or relocation assistance for the terminated individual. This will give you some leverage if you find yourself negotiating a mutually acceptable termination agreement.

Finally, your manager or a Personnel representative may give you a chance to practice conducting the termination interview. This practice will take some of the pressure off you and help you avoid misstatements that could be used against you later.

Step Three: Communicating the Decision

Communicating the termination decision to the employee is often the most difficult part of the whole process. Even if you have never conducted a termination interview, it is easy to see why it is difficult.

In communicating the decision, you must face an employee with whom you have not had a good relationship. Terminating an employee you like personally is even worse. In both cases, you may feel the need to justify your decision and you may even feel physically threatened.

This is a powerful set of concerns and you may be unsure of your ability to carry it off. If there is a positive force to balance these concerns, it is this: Employees who are on the verge of termination often sense the growing problem. Especially if you have done your groundwork in preparing for termination, employees are aware of the difficulty. In many cases, the final decision is a source of relief. The anxiety and waiting are over, and both you and the employee can get back to business.

When you are ready to communicate the termination decision, do so in a way that preserves the individual's dignity and self-worth. Begin by picking a private location where you won't be overheard and where there will be no observers. This may pose special problems if you feel physically threatened. Fortunately these cases are relatively rare, but you should be sure to protect yourself. It may be wise to have a security guard standing by, discreetly out of sight.

When you communicate your decision, be brief and to the point. Avoid lengthy discussions. Establish the mindset that you are not here to argue with the employee. Some will attempt to negotiate a second chance but you should not allow yourself to be dissuaded. Make it clear that the decision has already been made and there are no alternatives.

You also need to guard against complimenting the individual as a way of softening the blow. It may seem humane to comment on good things the employee has done or on the employee's potential in other roles. Unfortunately, these comments may place you in jeopardy if you are called into court. A former employee can easily take your remarks out of context, and a judge or jury might find it difficult to understand why you terminated an employee after saying good things about them.

Once you have communicated your decision, explain any severance benefits the employee will receive and explain the procedures to be followed. Give the employee as much time as is needed to regain composure. Allow the employee to gather up any personal belongings and to make a dignified exit.

Step Four: Following the Interview

There are three things you need to do following the interview. First, you need to document the interview. Company procedures may require you to fill out certain forms, but it is more common simply to write a memo to your files. Be sure to note the date of the interview, anything you promised the individual, and any threats or promises made by the individual. You may never need to refer to this memo, but it is good practice to have it on file. The memo serves to document the interview and may serve as a useful reminder if you are called to testify in any subsequent actions.

Informing other employees is the second thing you need to do following the interview. This can be a delicate process because you may be subject to legal action if you say derogatory things about the terminated individual. At the same time, informing other employees may be necessary to safeguard your facilities. The easiest way to deal with this dilemma is simply to announce that "effective today [employee's name] is no longer employed at this company."

This notice makes sure other employees know the employee is no longer free to move about your company's property. And, by avoiding discussion of the reasons, the notice keeps you clean. If anyone asks for details, simply say that it is inappropriate to discuss personnel matters.

Your final concern is responding to reference checks and other requests for information. You should expect the employee to be in the job market and one or more potential employers will probably call you for information. Here again, you face a potential conflict.

"No comment" doesn't seem appropriate, but anything you say about the employee could be grounds for a suit against you. The safest response is to verify that the person worked for you for a given period of time while explaining that you are not permitted to discuss personal information. You might say, "Our policy prohibits discussing personal information. However, I can verify that Jane Doe worked for us from January 19, 1986 through March 18, 1989."

Some callers may press for additional details and some can be very persistent. I recommend that you get yourself off the spot. Refer the caller to the Personnel Department and get back to business.

In summary, terminating an employee is seldom easy. Most of us find it very unpleasant—even when we know it is necessary. It often seems like a no-win situation because the very thing that makes a good manager—concern for people—seems to be in conflict with what needs to be done. The only consolation is doing it right; do it quickly, cleanly, and as humanely as possible. Protect yourself and your employer, and then get back to work.

Exit Interviews

Conducting exit interviews can also be difficult. Many managers take it personally when a valued employee informs them of the decision to quit. Of course, your emotions may range from "Oh, no! Why are you doing this?" to "Thank God, now I don't have to terminate this clown." In either case, and in all the cases in between, you need to think of the employee's decision to leave as a professional decision. They have made a career choice, and you need to respond appropriately.

Some organizations have developed formal exit interview procedures. Others have informal, commonsense procedures, and some have no set procedures at all. Whatever the case in your organization, you should still conduct a more-or-less formal exit interview with any of your subordinates who choose to quit.

"Why bother?" is a persistent question when exit interviews are discussed. There are three very good reasons for conducting exit interviews.

Reasons for Exit Interviews

Giving an employee a chance to reconsider is the first reason for conducting an exit interview. This can be important when the employee resigns in anger or haste. Think about some of your most valued employees. Many are important parts of your operation, but they may respond inappropriately to particularly frustrating situations. For example, the principal designer in one electronics firm has quit a half dozen times in the last few years. He really cares about his job and is easily frustrated when he doesn't get needed support on key projects. You may say that he is a bit of a prima donna, and you may be right. But the important point is that he is a uniquely talented designer, and the firm would suffer if he left. His supervisor has learned that the designer reconsiders when given a week or two to cool off. By the time the formal exit interview rolls around, the designer has already forgotten why he was ready to quit, and is back at work.

The designer is a unique individual, but there are other employees you may hope will reconsider. There is a severe shortage of skilled labor in many industries. Many managers try to retain their key people by making counteroffers whenever one announces plans to leave. Deciding whether or not to make a counteroffer depends on a number of factors. You need to ask yourself if you really want to keep the individual, how difficult it would be to replace them, and why they are planning to leave.

Employees who are leaving for greater opportunities, more challenging work, family reasons, or dissatisfaction with policies or procedures are unlikely to be swayed by a counteroffer. They may set up conditions that you cannot meet. On the other hand, a counteroffer may work when an employee is leaving only because of having received an offer with greater compensation. However, you need to be conscious of two concerns.

First, you may create problems for yourself if you routinely make counteroffers to employees who plan to leave. Your people will quickly see that threatening to leave is the best way to get a raise. You may soon find everyone in your organization spending more time looking for work than doing their jobs.

The second concern centers on the long-run prospects of keeping the employee. Some research has found that most employees who stay after receiving a counteroffer end up leaving their employers within a year anyway. If that is correct, making a counteroffer may be only a way of buying some additional time.

Gathering information is the second reason to conduct an exit interview. This is the most important reason, according to companies that have well-developed exit interview procedures. They believe that the information can be used to reduce turnover, establish fair pay scales, improve supervision and training, and correct unattractive working conditions. In other words, these companies use information from exit interviews to make sure that their normal procedures are working well.

These are useful objectives and could easily justify conducting exit interviews. However, you need to understand that former employees may not always tell the full story. Some are afraid that their bosses will give them poor references if they say anything negative about them. Others fear they would be "closing the door"—making it impossible for them to come back—if they say negative things about the company. A few will be anxious to avoid conflict or confrontation, and some may be too embarrassed to explain their personal reasons for leaving.

In spite of these reservations, you can still get useful information when you conduct the exit interview with care and tact.

Maintaining a personal relationship is the final reason for conducting exit interviews. Even though they won't be working for you any more, former employees may remain valuable contacts. They may steer new employees or customers to you. You may even be in a position to rehire them at some time in the future.

Conducting Exit Interviews

As you can see, there are good reasons for exit interviews. There are also some reasons to believe the employee may be reluctant to open up with you during the exit interview. This means that you need to schedule the interview carefully, explain why you are conducting it, create a favorable context, listen attentively to the employee's comments, and close on a positive note.

VOICES OF EXPERIENCE

Exit interviews are useful when:
1. departing employees know they will not be penalized for speaking freely
2. managers conducting the interviews take the process seriously
3. higher management takes a real interest in results of the interviews
4. the interviews are conducted at a time and place that encourages the departing employee to talk openly
5. questions and probes are used to solicit details
6. departing employees know the information they provide will be taken seriously by their manager and by higher management

---

Scheduling the interview is your first concern. Pick a time and place where the employee won't feel unduly pressured. Avoid the employee's last day at work because he or she will probably be preoccupied with check-out procedures and other personal concerns. Make sure the employee can talk freely in the location you've selected. Some managers prefer to take the employee out for a private lunch. Others use their office, the employee's office, or a conference room. These are all acceptable as long as you can talk without fear of being overheard.

The second step is explaining why you are conducting the interview. This doesn't have to be an elaborate introduction; you might use something as simple as the following.

Thank you for joining me for lunch. I know there is a lot on your mind but I wanted to have a little time with you before Friday.

We've worked together for a little over six years and I wanted you to know how much I've appreciated your help. We could never have managed the new semiconductor project without you.

I also have a selfish reason for inviting you to lunch. You know as much as anybody about what it's like to work for us and I wanted to get your reactions to some of the things that are going on.

But before we do that, let me summarize the benefits package that you will be taking with you.

This introduction is short and simple. And it leads logically into the third step. By summarizing the benefits the employee will receive, the manager has begun creating a favorable climate. Some employees may be reluctant to talk under any circumstances, but the more you can do to make them feel comfortable, the better your chances of getting useful information from them.

Formal exit interviews use structured interview guides. You might want to develop one if your company doesn't already have a formal exit procedure. However, you may be able to learn just about as much if you begin with some fairly general questions and listen attentively to the employee's answers. You might use some of the following open questions.

Why don't you tell me a little bit about your new job?
What do you find most attractive about the new job?
How does it differ fom your job here?
What did you like most about working for us?
What did you like least about your job here?

Most employees will be ready and able to answer these questions, especially if your nonverbal behavior shows that you are really interested in their answers. If you sense the employee is nervous, you might substitute indirect questions. For example, you could use the following instead of those listed above.

What's the new company like?
What do the people there find attractive about their work?
What do you think our people like most about working here?
What do you think they like least about working here?

The important feature of these indirect questions is that they take the person off the spot. The individual can answer in terms of his or her own experiences without appearing to criticize you or the company.

Closing on a positive note is the final step. Thank the employee for the interview, say something positive about the new job, and wish the person luck. The following example may seem artificial because it is out of context. In a real situation, it would probably work well.

> Well, John, our time is just about up. Thank you for joining me. The chance to develop a new program sounds really exciting. I'd like it if you would let me know how things are going from time to time. Good luck!

Conclusion

Change is a constant element in our personal and professional lives. In professional situations, change often means bringing employment relationships to an end. Sometimes employees choose to leave and sometimes managers are forced to terminate them. Whatever the reason, the manager's final contact with the employee often determines the course of the postemployment relationship. Today's managers need to be prepared to conduct both termination and exit interviews.

Employment law is a complicated field, and you should always consult an attorney before doing anything that may expose you to legal jeopardy. The general principle governing employment is an "at will" doctrine. This means that employment is a voluntary relationship that may be terminated by either the employer or the employee. There are several exceptions to this doctrine and you may be required to demonstrate good cause whenever firing an employee would be contrary to public policy, violate a contract or implied agreement, be inconsistent with "good faith and fair dealing" expectations, or involve members of protected classes.

It is never easy to fire an employee, but you can simplify the process by dividing it into four steps: (1) justifying the termination, (2) consulting higher management and getting needed approvals, (3) communicating the message, and (4) following through after the termination.

Exit interviews are interviews with employees who have chosen to leave of their own accord. There are several reasons to conduct exit interviews, and the most important include giving the employee an opportunity to reconsider, gathering information that may help you reduce turnover, and maintaining an ongoing relationship even after the employee has left.

Exit interviews can be informal but they should not be so casual that departing employees do not take them seriously. Pick a time and place where employees won't feel unduly pressured, explain why you are conducting the interview, and close on a positive note.

The case following this chapter puts you in the place of JoAnn Anderson, manager of a computer programming support group in a large corporation. Three of her twelve employees have been called to her attention for employment-related reasons and you need to decide how you would deal with them. Two appear to be destined for termination while the other one has chosen to quit. Their profiles raise a variety of issues. Using the information provided, plan to conduct the necessary termination and exit interviews. Remember that you may not have adequate information to justify termination and you may need to find another alternative. If someone is available to help, you may choose to act out the roles of manager and employee.

Suggested Readings

Condon, Thomas J., and Richard H. Wolff. "Procedures That Safeguard Your Right to Fire." *Harvard Business Review* (November–December 1985: 19–21.

Corbett, Laurence P. "Avoiding Wrongful Discharge Suits." *Management Solutions* (June 1986): 19–23.

Coulson, Robert. *The Termination Handbook.* New York: The Free Press, 1981.

Drost, Donald A., Fabius P. O'Brien, and Steve Marsh. "Exit Interviews: Master the Possibilities." *Personnel Administrator* (February 1987): 104–110.

Gilberg, Kenneth R., and Philip R. Voluck. "Employee Termination Without Litigation." *Personnel* (May 1987): 17–19.

Case Study

JoAnn Anderson manages the computer programming support group in a large corporation. She has been in her position for a little over three months and has begun to get acquainted with the twelve programmers who report to her. All are well educated and have the training appropriate for their roles. The files available to her include the employees' work histories, and she has spent a good deal of time reviewing records of past performance appraisals. The company has used the same appraisal system for several years, and each programmer is periodically evaluated in three areas: (1) project completion, including time required and subjective quality, (2) interpersonal skills, focusing on their interaction with internal clients, and (3) professional development.

JoAnn is just beginning to feel comfortable in her new role, but three employees have been called to her attention. The first, Barbara Allen, is an outstanding employee and has received several offers from other companies. The other two, Harold Johnson and Carol Smith, are "marginal" employees and JoAnn is beginning to think about terminating them. Put yourself in JoAnn's place and see how you would respond to each of the three.

Barbara Allen

Barbara is a 32-year-old single mother with three children, ages 4, 6, and 7. She has been with the company for seven years, and her performance evaluations have been outstanding on all counts. Her current salary is one of the highest in the group because she has received the maximum raise possible for the last five years. Barbara is pleased with her salary but has recently voiced concern about the medical and dental benefits provided. Several firms have tried to lure Barbara away with promises of increased benefits. She has recently received an attractive offer from another company. The offer includes a salary slightly above her current one, but nearly double the medical and dental coverage. More important, in her eyes, the other firm provides free child care for all of their employees.

Barbara has thought about the offer and notified JoAnn that she intends to resign at the end of the month.

Harold Johnson

Harold is a 45-year-old man who has been with the company for four years. He is divorced but supporting three minor children from two previous marriages. His current salary is just about average for the group, and this is consistent with his perceived performance for the last few years. In fact, he has been rated "average" in every category on the annual appraisals for the entire time he has been with the company.

Harold has a serious temper and he has been written up a number of times. He seems to bully or intimidate clients and has been reprimanded seven times. His file includes three personal warnings and four formal notices. Five of the managers JoAnn's group supports have asked her to assign other programmers to their projects.

JoAnn was careful to assign Harold to projects requiring little interpersonal communication. In the last week she has received two memos that she cannot ignore. The first came from a senior manager in another area and the second from one of Harold's current clients. Both describe Harold as a "time bomb looking for a place to explode," and both ask JoAnn to replace him immediately.

JoAnn knows that her job depends on keeping her group's clients happy. Unfortunately, all of her programmers are assigned to specific projects and reassigning Harold would place a real strain on her operation.

Carol Smith

Carol Smith is in her early 50s. She has been with the company for over twenty years, beginning as a secretary and transferring into the programming support group after completing a series of night-school courses in computer programming.

Carol is married and has three children who have finished school and are now on their own. She is the only black in JoAnn's group and one of the few in the company. Her work has always been below average—near the bottom of the second quartile according to the performance evaluation records. Curiously, her salary is above average for the group because she has been with the company so long and because she received a large but unexplained raise four years ago.

JoAnn has been reviewing Carol's record because she is clearly the weakest member of the group. There are no specific problems but JoAnn is confident she can replace Carol with someone who is younger, more skilled, and less expensive.

Index

A
Agendas, meetings, 80–81
Analytical style
  characteristics of, 14
  time for use of, 15–16
Annual appraisal form, performance
  appraisal, 139

B
Behavioral style
  characteristics of, 15
  time for use of, 16
Businesses, new work strategies,
  144–147

C
Career goals, job applicant, 43
Central tendency problem, performance appraisal, 120
Civil Rights Act of 1964, 34
Clarification, as interview probe, 49
Coaching
  relationship to delegation, 69–71,
   82
  rules for teaching, 70
  steps in process, 69–70

Communication, importance in management, 9, 10–11
Communication styles
  analytical style, 14
  behavioral style, 15
  case studies, 20–25
  consultative style, 14–15
  directive style, 13–14
  as habit, 11
  inventory for, 11–13
  time for use of, 15–18
Compromise strategy, negotiation,
  148, 149–150
Conflict
  approaches to, 147–148
  See also Negotiation.
Confrontation, as interview probe,
  50
Consultative style
  characteristics of, 14–15
  time for use of, 16
Credentials of job applicant,
  40–45
  appearance of, 41
  career goals and, 43
  checklist for, 44

Credentials of job applicant *(Cont.)*
  missing information, 41–42
  red flags, 42, 43
  reference check, 51–52
  work history, 42–43
Criticism
  coping with, 131–132
  defensive reactions to, 129

D
Defensive reaction, 129
Delegation, 61–90
  case studies, 84–90
  definition of, 69
  job expectancy scale, 71–75, 79
  learning to delegate, 63–66
  levels of responsibility, 72–74
  main factors in, 72
  meetings and, 80–82
  new approaches to, 62–63
  relationship to coaching, 69–71, 82
  teams and, 76–80
Directive style
  characteristics of, 13–14
  time for use of, 15

E
Elaboration, as interview probe, 48–49
Employment at will doctrine, 176–177
Employment interview, 30–31, 35–40, 45
  closed-ended questions, 39
  common questions asked, 38
  direct questions, 39–40
  final candidates, categories of, 50–51
  indirect questions, 40
  interview guide, 35–37
  interview probes, use of, 47–50
  introductory stage of, 37
  open-ended questions, 39
  place for, 45
  problems in interviewee's responses, 46
  time allotment for, 45
Equal Employment Opportunity Act of 1972, 34
Exit interviews, 182–186
  conducting interview, 185–186
  reasons for, 183–185

F
Feedback
  effective feedback, characteristics of, 130–131
  manner of communication and, 129
  in performance appraisal, 128–131
  value of, 128

H
Halo error, performance appraisal, 120–121
Hostile subordinate, 101–102

I
Internal summaries, as interview probe, 48
Interview probes, 47–50
  clarification, 49
  confrontation, 50
  elaboration, 48–49
  internal summaries, 48
  mirror statements, 47
  neutral phases, 47–48
  repetition, 49–50
  silent attention, 47
Interviews
  performance appraisal interview, 125–127, 133–135
  See also Employment interview.

J
Job description, 32–34
Job expectancy scale, 71–75, 79
  delegation/coaching and, 74–75
  levels of subordinate responsibility, 72–74
Job interview. *See* Employment interview.
Job turnover
  costs of, 31
  reducing turnover, 174
  See also Terminations.

L
Labor unions, 145
Lazy subordinate, 100–101
Legal issues
  employment at will doctrine, 176–177
  former employees, 174–178
Leniency error, performance appraisal, 119–120

M
Management
    challenges of, 2–4
    rewards for success, 2
    team approach, 3
Managers
    career path, 5–7
    communication, importance of, 9,
        10–11
    delegation, problem of, 8–9
    relationship building and, 9–10
    role of, 66–68
    time problem of, 8
Meetings
    agendas, 80–81
    limiting time of, 81–82
    team approach and, 79–82
Mirror statements, as interview probe,
    47
Missions, and motivation, 97–98
Motivation
    case example, 113–116
    identifying employees' motives, 96–
        97
    lack of motivation, example of, 95–
        96
    missions and, 97–98
    opportunity to achieve and, 98–
        100

N
Negotiation
    case studies, 164–165
    compromise strategy, 148, 149–150
    concluding negotiation session,
        157–159
    conflict, approaches to, 147–148
    example of, 142–143
    hard ball tactics, 147
    negotiation session procedure, 154–
        157
    negotiation tactics, 159–161
    new work structures and, 144–147
    pre-negotiation session, 151–154
    problem solving strategy, 148, 150–
        151
    showdowns and, 150
    win-win strategies, 148–149
Neutral phases, as interview probe,
    47-48
New employees
    candidates' expectations, 34–35

case study, 55–60
credentials of applicant, 40–45
employment interview, 30–31, 35–
    40, 45
job description, 32–34
managerial role in, 27, 30
problems of, 28–30
reference check, 51–52

O
Opportunity to achieve, and motiva-
    tion, 98–100
Organizations
    power and politics in, 161–163
    systems approach to, 67–68
Ownership of resources, 145–146

P
Performance appraisal, 104
    annual appraisal form, 139
    audiences for, 122–124
    case example, 137–140
    central tendency problem, 120
    criticism, coping with, 131–132
    difficult employee responses to,
        132–133
    feedback in, 128–131
    halo error, 120–121
    interview, 125–127, 133–135
    leniency error, 119–120
    solutions to problems of, 121–122
    strategies for, 124–128
    unpopularity of, 118–119
Performance problems
    common types of, 92–93, 94–95
    hostile subordinate, 101–102
    ineffective teams, 102–103
    lazy subordinate, 100–101
    origin of, 93–94
    personal development conferences
        and, 103–107
    strategies for solution to, 107
    team building and, 107–111
Personal development conferences,
    103–107
    procedure for, 104–107
Politics and business
    organizations and, 161–163
    power persuasion tactics, 145
Power persuasion tactics, 145
Problem solving strategy, negotiation,
    148, 150–151

R
Reference check, 51–52
  closing, 52–53
  introduction, 51–52
  and terminations, 182
  verification aspect, 52
Relationship building, and managers,
    9–10
Repetition, as interview probe, 49–50
Responsibility, levels for subordinates,
    72–74

S
Self-fulfilling prophecies, 127
Silent attention, as interview probe, 47
Subordinates
  coaching of, 69–71
  levels of responsibility, 72–74
  performance problems, 92–95,
    100–103

T
Task-related problems, 16
Team approach, 76–80
  benefits/limitations of, 76–77, 78
  concerns/problems of team, 109–
    110

delegation process and, 77–79
effectiveness of, 76
ineffective team, problem of, 102–
    103
management, 3
mature teams, characteristics of, 79
meetings and, 79–82
Team building, procedure in, 107–111
Terminations
  case study, 189–191
  communicating termination decision,
    180–181
  documentation and, 178, 181–182
  exit interviews, 182–186
  former employees, impact on com-
    pany, 174–175
  higher management, involvement of,
    179–180
  justification of, 179
  legal issues, 174–178
  notice to other employees, 182
  reference checks and, 182

W
Win-win strategies, negotiation, 148–
    149
Work history, job applicant, 42–43